Knitted Comfort for the Sole

the art of everyday living

Vice President and Chief Operations Officer: Tom Siebenmorgen
Vice President, Sales and Marketing: Pam Stebbins
Vice President, Operations: Jim Dittrich
Managing Editor: Susan White Sullivan
Director of Designer Relations: Debra Nettles
Senior Art Director: Rhonda Shelby
Senior Prepress Director: Mark Hawkins

Produced for Leisure Arts, Inc. by Penn Publishing Ltd.
www.penn.co.il
Editor: Shoshana Brickman
Design and layout: Ariane Rybski
Technical editing: Rita Greenfeder
Photography by: Danya Weiner and Liah Chesnokov

PRINTED IN THE U.S.A.

ISBN: 9781601403292
Library of Congress Control Number: 2008943610

Cover photography by Danya Weiner

Knitted Comfort for the Sole

22 Innovative Designs for Socks, Slippers, & More

by

LENA MAIKON

A LEISURE ARTS PUBLICATION

Contents

Introduction 6

General Instructions 7

Abbreviation Charts 9

Materials and Tools 11

Anatomy of the Sock 12

DESIGNS

Classic Striped Socks 14

Snow Falling on Socks 20

Dancing Queen Socks 24

The Truck Stops Here Socks 27

Super Shoesocks 32

Zingy Zigzag Socks 37

Diamond Delight 40

Wonderland of Wool Socks 44

Traditionally Cable Socks 50

Summer Net Socks 54

Wavy Sea Socks 58

Cute as a Bunny Cuffed Socks 62

Totally Toe Socks 66

Mary's Little Lamb Socks 71

Square Crocheted Knee Socks 76

Fluffy Slippers 80

Mutt-ering Around Slippers 84

Autumn Slippers 89

Laced Legwarmers 94

Sally's Seashell Crocheted Socks 99

Apple of Your Eye Socks 104

Fluffy Legwarmers 110

ENHANCEMENTS

Crocheted Flower 114

Lucky Leather Sock Pocket 116

Hemp Leaf Ribbon 118

Pompon on a String 120

Funny Bunnies 122

Rosebud Ribbon 124

Sole Templates 126

Introduction

Socks. They keep feet warm, dry, and cozy, providing a comforting layer between your foot and the outside world. Some people wear socks all day, every day. Other people save socks for wintertime. Some people love thick, fluffy socks. Other people prefer delicate, elegant socks. Whatever your sock preference, you're sure to find something to suit your fancy—and your foot—in this book!

This book contains patterns for summer socks, winter socks, short socks, and knee socks. There are socks for boys and socks for girls, socks for serious people and socks with a sense of silliness. There are several sets of slippers, too, for keeping feet cozy while padding around the house, and a couple of legwarmer projects that are ideal for dressing up (and warming up) your legs. There are also several enhancement projects: knitted or crocheted add-ons for dressing up handmade or store-bought socks.

In addition to making different styles of socks, the projects in this book also use a variety of different stitches and techniques. Some projects are knitted using two standard knitting needles; others use five double-pointed needles; several include crocheted accents.

If this is your first time knitting socks, you'll find the Anatomy of the Sock section (page 12) particularly helpful. A classic sock design complete with detailed explanations can be found on pages 14 to 19. If you're not quite ready to make a pair of socks yet, or if you're just looking for a way to spruce up a pair of readymade socks, try making one of the enhancement projects and adding it to a pair you've already got. Experienced knitters looking for a little challenge will find that here too, in sock projects that include open gussets, intricate patterns, and diverse stitches.

ABOUT THE AUTHOR

Lena Maikon learned to knit from her grandmother at the age of five in her hometown of Novosibrisk, Russia. She didn't pick up her knitting needles for thirty years, but started to knit again as a form of creative therapy. This quickly turned into a passion and profession. Lena often uses unconventional materials in her designs, and dreams of creating a knitted world. She knits and crochets socks, shoes, dresses, handbags, flowers, vases, and light fixtures. She has published two creative knitting books, and has her own handmade clothing and accessory label, **Leninka**. Lena is the mother of two sons who love to wear fuzzy knitted sweaters and cozy socks.

General Instructions

Standard Yarn Weight System

Yarn Weight Symbol & Names	LACE **0**	SUPER FINE **1**	FINE **2**	LIGHT **3**	MEDIUM **4**	BULKY **5**	SUPER BULKY **6**
Type of Yarns in Category	Fingering, size 10 crochet thread	Sock, Fingering, Baby	Sport, Baby	DK, Light Worsted	Worsted, Afghan, Aran	Chunky, Craft, Rug	Bulky, Roving
Knit Gauge Range* in Stockinette St to 4" (10 cm)	33-40** sts	27-32 sts	23-26 sts	31-24 sts	16-20 sts	12-15 sts	6-11 sts
Advised Needle Size Range	000-1	1 to 3	3 to 5	5 to 7	7 to 9	9 to 11	11 and larger

*GUIDELINES ONLY: The chart above reflects the most commonly used gauges and needle sizes for specific yarn categories.

** Lace weight yarns are usually knitted on larger needles to create lacy openwork patterns. Accordingly, a gauge range is difficult to determine. Always follow the gauge stated in your pattern.

KNIT TERMINOLOGY	
United States	**International**
gauge	tension
bind off	cast off
yarn over (YO)	yarn forward (yfwd) or yarn around needle (yrn)

CROCHET TERMINOLOGY	
United States	**International**
slip stitch (slip st)	single crochet (sc)
single crochet (sc)	double crochet (dc)
half double crochet (hdc)	half treble crochet (htc)
double crochet (dc)	treble crochet (tr)
treble crochet (tr)	double treble crochet (dtr)
treble double crochet (dtr)	triple treble crochet (ttr)
triple treble crochet (tr tr)	quadruple treble crochet (qtr)
skip	miss

Fit Charts

MAN'S FIT CHART					
Sock Size	EXTRA SMALL	SMALL	MEDIUM	LARGE	EXTRA LARGE
Shoe Size	4/5	6/7	8/9	10/11	12/13

WOMAN'S FIT CHART					
Sock Size	EXTRA SMALL	SMALL	MEDIUM	LARGE	EXTRA LARGE
Shoe Size	4/5	6/7	8/9	10/11	12/13

SKILL LEVELS

⬤▭▭▭ BEGINNER	Projects for first-time knitters using basic knit and purl stitches. Minimal shaping.
⬤⬤▭▭ EASY	Projects using basic stitches, repetitive stitch patterns, simple color changes, and simple shaping and finishing.
⬤⬤⬤▭ INTERMEDIATE	Projects with a variety of stitches, such as basic cables and lace, simple intarsia, double-pointed needles and knitting in the round needle techniques, mid-level shaping and finishing.
⬤⬤⬤⬤ EXPERIENCED	Projects using advanced techniques and stitches, such as short rows, fair isle, more intricate intarsia, cables, lace patterns, and numerous color changes.

KNITTING NEEDLES

U.S.	0	1	2	3	4	5	6	7	8	9	10	10½	11	13	15	17
U.K.	13	12	11	10	9	8	7	6	5	4	3	2	1	00	000	---
METRIC - MM	2	2.25	2.75	3.25	3.5	3.75	4	4.5	5	5.5	6	6.5	8	9	10	12.75

CROCHET HOOKS

U.S.	B-1	C-2	D-3	E-4	F-5	G-6	H-7	I-9	J-10	K-10½	N	P	Q
METRIC - MM	2.25	2.75	3.25	3.5	3.75	4	5	5.5	6	6.5	9	10	15

Basics

MAKE TWO

For every project, follow the pattern twice (for left and right sock) unless otherwise specified.

SIZE

The sock size given for all projects was obtained by measuring the length of the foot of the sock or slipper, from the heel flap to the toe (see Anatomy of the Sock, page 12), and converting this measurement into standard shoe sizes (see Fit Charts, page 7).

If you are knitting for feet that are a little longer or wider than average, you may need to adjust the pattern by adding stitches or rows to the foot of the sock. With a little practice, you'll find yourself able to make socks that fit perfectly the first time, every time.

LENGTH ON LEG

This indicates where the sock will end on the leg. In many patterns, you can make the sock as high or low as you like.

ENHANCEMENTS

These decorative additions include animal faces, delicate ribbons, pockets, and colorful flowers, made from diverse materials such as beads, buttons, and leather. Each enhancement is suited to a specific sock project, but can just as well be added to store-bought socks or any other pair of handmade socks.

Abbreviation Charts

KNITTING ABBREVIATIONS

*	repeat instructions following the single asterisk as directed
beg	begin
BO	bind off
cont	continue
dec	decrease
dpn	double-pointed needles
inc	increase
k or K	knit
k1inc1	knit 1 increase 1
k2tog	knit 2 stitches together
p or P	purl
p2tog	purl 2 stitches together
prev	previous
rem	remaining
rep	repeat
rnd (s)	round (s)
RS	right side
skp	skip
sl	slip
St st	stockinette stitch
tog	together
WS	wrong side
yo	yarn over

CROCHET ABBREVIATIONS

*	repeat instructions following the single asterisk as directed
ch	chain stitch
cont	continue
dc	double crochet
hdc	half double crochet
rem	remaining
rnd (s)	round (s)
sc	single crochet
sk	skip
sl st	slip stitch
tr	triple crochet

PATTERN STITCHES

K1   knit 1

P1   purl 1

YO   yarn over

k2tog   knit 2 stitches together

SKPO   slip 1, knit 1, pass slipped stitch over

Double Left-Slanting Decrease   Slip stitch to right needle, knit 2 stitches together, pass slipped stitch over 2 stitches.

Cross 2 Left   Slip next stitch onto cable needle and hold at front of work, knit next stitch from left-hand needle, then knit stitch from cable needle.

Cross 2 Right   Slip next stitch onto cable needle and hold at back of work, knit next stitch from left-hand needle, then knit stitch from cable needle.

Cross 2 Left on Purl   Slip next stitch onto cable needle and hold at front of work, purl next stitch from left-hand needle, then knit stitch from cable needle.

Cross 2 Right on Purl   Slip next stitch onto cable needle and hold at back of work, knit next stitch from left-hand needle, then purl stitch from cable needle.

Cross 4 Left   Slip next 2 stitches onto cable needle and leave at front of work, knit next 2 stitches from left-hand needle, then knit stitches from cable needle.

Cross 4 Right   Slip next 2 stitches onto cable needle and leave at back of work, knit next 2 stitches from left-hand needle, then knit stitches from cable needle.

Cable Twist   Slip next 3 stitches onto cable needle and hold at front of work, knit next 3 stitches from left-hand needle, then knit stitches from cable needle.

MC   Main color

CC   Complimentary color

N   Apple Pattern

Materials and Tools

You'll need a few basic materials and tools for knitting socks. Materials such as leather, beads, and buttons can be found at most general craft stores. Yarn, needles, and crochet hooks can be found at some craft stores and of course knitting shops. The internet is an excellent source for finding all of these items.

YARN

The specific yarns chosen for the projects in this book complement the style of each individual pair of socks. If you can't find exactly the same brand or type, or if you'd like to experiment, just keep a few basic pointers in mind.

- Select yarns that won't prickle, scratch, or irritate your feet.

- You will (literally) walk all over your projects, so select yarns that are sturdy and washable.

- If you are making socks to wear with shoes, select a yarn that isn't too thick.

- If you are making slippers, select a yarn that is particularly durable.

- Be sure to select high-quality yarns, as you will really want these socks to last.

BUTTONS, BEADS, AND BELLS

These are used to add decorative touches. Though the size and color are specified in each project, feel free to adjust as desired.

HOLDERS

These are used to hold stitches while other stitches are being worked.

LEATHER HOLE PUNCH

This is used to punch holes in leather pieces.

LEATHER LACES

These are used to tie up socks and slippers, and to add decorative touches.

LEATHER PIECES

These are used to make sturdy soles on slippers.

NEEDLES AND HOOKS

Some of the projects use basic single-pointed knitting needles. Others use a set of five double-pointed needles, or cable needles. Several projects include crocheted enhancements that are made using a single crochet hook. Many projects use more than one set of needles.

SCISSORS

Use these to cut yarn, thread, and templates.

SEWING NEEDLE AND THREAD

These are used to sew on buttons, beads, and other adornments. Be sure to use sturdy thread so that the adornments are sewed on securely.

STITCH MARKER

This is used to mark stitches while you work.

TAPESTRY NEEDLE

This is used to sew seams. Make sure the eye of the needle is wide enough to thread the yarn.

TRACING PAPER, PENCIL, AND PERMANENT MARKER

These are used to copy templates and transfer them to leather or cardboard.

Anatomy of the Sock

Though socks may come in a wide variety of shapes and sizes, most socks have the same basic parts. For detailed instructions on how to knit a basic sock that includes all of these elements, see the Classic Striped Socks project (page 14).

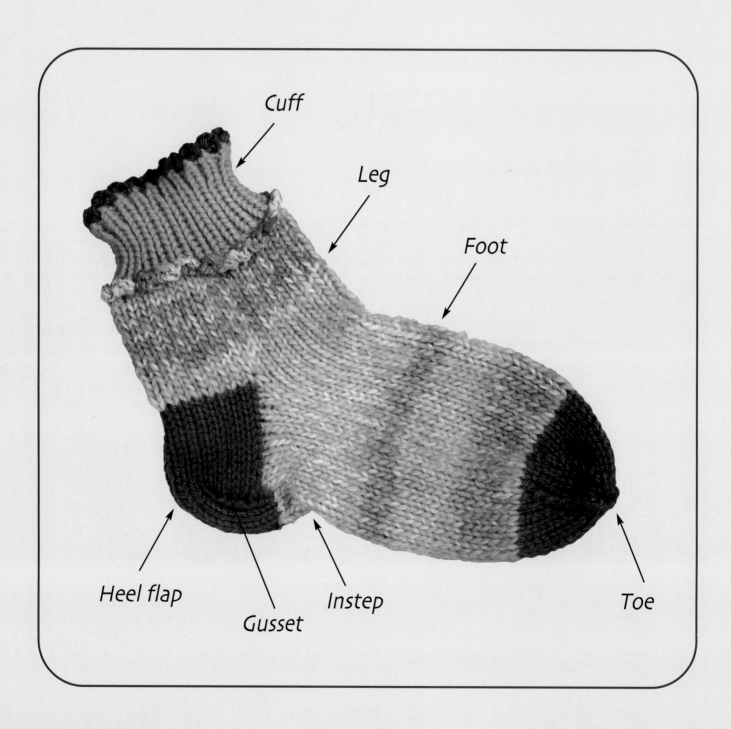

DESIGNS

In the following pages, you'll find patterns for a wide variety of sock styles. Choose different colors of yarns to create different looks, and dress up the designs using the enhancement described in the second part of the book.

Classic Striped Socks

Every sock drawer should have at least one pair of striped socks. This basic design is a great pattern for beginners. Make a pair for all the special feet in your life!

EXPERIENCE LEVEL

■■□□ EASY

SIZES

Woman's small (woman's medium, woman's large, man's small, man's medium, man's large)

LENGTH ON LEG

Above the ankle

MATERIALS AND TOOLS

Yarn A **MEDIUM 4** : 127 (156, 196, 225, 255, 294)yd/116 (144 180, 207, 234, 270)m of Medium weight yarn, wool/acrylic, in variegated orange and green

Yarn B **SUPER FINE 1** : 66yd/60m of Superfine weight yarn, wool/acrylic/superwash cashmere, in orange

Yarn C **SUPER FINE 1** : 147yd/134m of Superfine weight yarn, wool/acrylic/superwash cashmere, in green

Yarn D **MEDIUM 4** : 16yd/15m of Medium weight yarn, cotton/nylon/polyester, in variegated orange and yellow
Knitting needles: Set of 5 dpn, 4 mm (size 6 U.S.) *or size to obtain gauge*
Crochet hook: 3.5 mm (E/4)
Scissors
Tapestry needle

GAUGE

10 sts and 14 rows = 2"/5cm with Yarn A in Stockinette Stitch
10 sts and 16 rows = 2"/5cm with Yarn B in Rib Stitch
Always take time to check your gauge.

Instructions

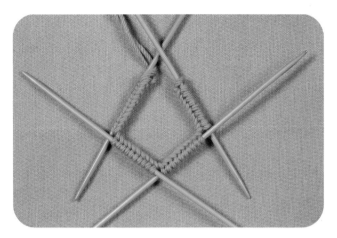

Figure 1

Figure 2

CUFF

With Yarn B, CO 36 (40, 44, 48, 52, 56) sts.

If you tend to cast on too tight, cast your stitches onto a wider needle first, then transfer the stitches to the needles you'll be using for the socks.

Divide sts evenly between 4 needles—9 (10, 11, 12, 13, 14) sts on each needle. Join, taking care not to twist sts on needles. The space between Needles 1 and 4 is the center of the sock. (Figure 1)

NOTE: *To join, connect the round by knitting the stitches from Needle 1 after the stitches from Needle 4.*

Work around in k1, p1 rib for 15 (15, 20, 25, 30, 35) rnds, or desired length to beg of leg. Cut Yarn B.

LEG

Do you prefer knee socks, ankle socks, or something in between? This is the stage to decide, as you'll be knitting even until the heel flap.

Join Yarn A, and work around in St st (k all sts) for 15 (15, 20, 25, 30, 35) rnds, or desired length to beg of heel flap. End at Needle 3. Don't cut yarn (you'll be using it again to work the gusset).

HEEL FLAP

Rows are worked on Needles 1 and 4 to make the heel of the sock. Rows at the top of the foot are left untouched for now.

Join Yarn C and using spare needle, sl 1, k across sts from Needle 4, then Needle 1—17 (19, 21, 23, 25, 27) sts; leave sts on Needles 2 and 3 unworked.

Work back and forth in St st (k1 row, p1 row) for 13 (15, 15, 17, 19, 21) more rows. End with WS row. (Figure 2)

HEEL

Now you'll work short rows to decrease stitches, shaping the heel.

Work short rows as follows:

Sl 1, k10 (12, 13, 14, 16, 18), skp, turn;

*sl 1, p 4 (6, 6, 6, 8, 8), p2tog, turn;

sl 1, k4 (6, 6, 6, 8, 8), skp, turn.

Rep from * until all sts have been worked—6 (8, 8, 8, 10, 10) sts on your needle (Figure 3). Cut Yarn C.

Next row (RS): With Yarn A, k3 (4, 4, 4, 5, 5) sts onto Needle 4, then k3 (4, 4, 4, 5, 5) sts onto Needle 1.

Figure 3

GUSSET

Increase stitches to make up for those that were decreased when turning the heel. These stitches will accommodate the width of the foot, so if you are knitting for an especially wide foot, take that into account now.

Using Needle 1, insert the needle into 1st k st from the edge and pick up and k10 (10, 11, 12, 12, 13) sts evenly spaced along edge of heel (Figure 4)

NOTE: *When forming the gusset, avoid holes between the corner of the heel flap and the leg in the following manner. For the last stitch that you pick up, insert the needle into the 2nd row stitch under the 1st stitch on Needle 2. For the 1st st that you pick up, insert the needle into the 2nd row stitch under the 1st sts on Needle 4.*

Cont to work in-the-rnd and k sts on Needles 2 and 3.

Using spare needle, pick up and k10 (10, 11, 12, 12, 13) sts evenly spaced along edge of heel, then k3 (4, 4, 4, 5, 5) sts from Needle 4—13 (14, 15, 16, 17, 18) sts on Needles 1 and 4.

Figure 4

INSTEP

Now you are forming the curve of the sock. You'll be decreasing stitches back to the original amount.

*Rnd 1: K all sts.

Rnd 2: Needle 1: K to last 3 sts, skp, k1; Needles 2 and 3: K all sts; Needle 4: K1, k2tog, k to end.

Rep from * four times, until there are 9 (10, 11, 12, 13, 14) sts on Needles 1 and 4—36 (40, 44, 48, 52, 56) sts total.

FOOT

Here you are knitting to fit the foot, from the heel until the beginning of the toe. If the foot you are knitting for is particularly long, take this into account now.

Work around in k for 30 (32, 36, 40, 48, 56) rnds, or desired length to beg of toe. Cut Yarn A.

TOE

Socks are tapered to fit snugly around toes. Decrease stitches here until you are ready to finish.

Join Yarn C.

*Rnd 1: K all sts.

Rnd 2 (dec rnd): Needles 1 and 3: K to last 3 sts, skp, k1; Needles 2 and 4: K1, k2tog, k to end.

Rep from * until 5 (6, 7, 8, 9, 10) sts rem on each needle.

Now rep rnd 2 every rnd until 3 sts rem on each needle.

Cut yarn, leaving a 10"/25cm tail. Thread the needle with the tail and *insert through all sts, from 1st to last. Draw yarn back through all sts and tighten. Rep from * twice. Cut yarn, tie ends, and hide tails. (Figure 5)

Figure 5

Finishing

CROCHETED EDGING

Cuff top

With RS facing, top of cuff away from you, and Yarn C, insert hook under 1st CO st and ch 3, hdc 1 under same st.

*Sk, then sc 1, ch 2, hdc 1 under same st. Rep from * all around cuff.

Sl st into 2nd ch from beg. Cut yarn, tie ends, and hide tails.

Cuff bottom

With RS facing, bottom of cuff away from you, and Yarn D, insert hook through a p st on last rnd of cuff and ch 3, hdc 1 through same st.

*Sk, then sc 1, ch 2, hdc 1 through same st. Rep from * all around cuff.

Sl st into 2nd ch from beg. Cut yarn, tie ends, and hide tails. (Figure 6)

Figure 6

This project was knit with

(A) 2 (2, 2, 3, 3, 3) balls of Gedifra Fashion Trend Stripe, 51% wool/49% acrylic yarn, heavy worsted weight, 1¾oz/50g = approx 98yd/90m per ball, color #4622

(B) 1 ball of Gedifra Cashmerino, 58% wool/30% acrylic/12% superwash cashmere yarn, fingering weight, 1¾oz/50g = approx 147yd/134m per ball, color #4822

(C) 1 ball of Gedifra Cashmerino, 58% wool/30% acrylic/12% superwash cashmere yarn, fingering weight, 1¾oz/50g = approx 147yd/134m per ball, color #4878

(D) 1 ball of Gedifra Fiocco Oro, 65% cotton/27% nylon/8% polyester yarn, heavy worsted weight, 1¾oz/50g = approx 76yd/59m per ball, color #6603

Snow Falling on Socks

With the wintry fringe on these socks, you'll have a fresh blanket of snow at your feet regardless of the weather forecast. There is no heel flap on this sock, making it a great design for new knitters.

EXPERIENCE LEVEL

■■□□ EASY

SIZES

Woman's small (woman's medium, woman's large)

LENGTH ON LEG

Lower calf

MATERIALS AND TOOLS

Yarn A **MEDIUM 4** : 147 (196, 245)yd/135 (180, 225)m of Medium weight yarn, wool/acrylic, in beige and white

Yarn B **BULKY 5** : 109yd/100m of Bulky weight yarn, merino wool/acrylic/polyamide, in cream

Yarn C **SUPER BULKY 6** : 4yd/4m of Super bulky weight yarn, wool, in cream

Yarn D **MEDIUM 4** : 26yd/24m of Medium weight yarn, mohair/acrylic, in gray-brown

Yarn E **MEDIUM 4** : 26yd/24m of Medium weight yarn, mohair/acrylic, in burgundy

Yarn F **MEDIUM 4** : 26yd/24m of Medium weight yarn, mohair/acrylic, in olive green

Knitting needles: Set of 5 dpn, 4 mm (size 6 U.S.) *or size to obtain gauge*

Crochet hook: 3.5 mm (E/4)

Scissors

Tapestry needle

GAUGE

11 sts and 13 rows = 2"/5cm with Yarn A in Stockinette Stitch

Always take time to check your gauge.

Instructions

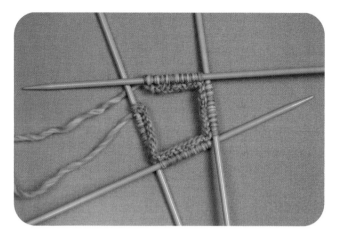

Figure 1

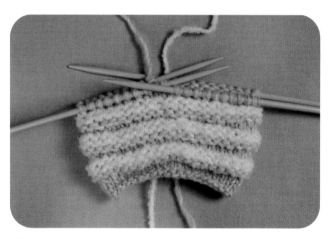

Figure 2

Figure 3

LEG

With Yarn A, CO 40 (44, 48) sts.

Divide sts evenly between 4 needles—10 (11, 12) sts on each needle (Figure 1).

K all sts for 4 rnds.

Join Yarn B and p all sts for 3 rnds.

*With Yarn A, k all sts for 3 rnds.

With Yarn B, p all sts for 3 rnds.

Rep from * five (six, six) times, or desired length to beg of foot (Figure 2). Cut Yarn B.

FOOT

With Yarn A, p all sts for 50 (55, 60) rnds, or desired length to beg of toe.

TOE

Join Yarn B.

*Rnd 1: K all sts.

Rnd 2 (dec rnd): Needles 1 and 3: K to last 3 sts, skp, k1. Needles 2 and 4: K1, k2tog, k to end.

Rep from * until 5 (6, 7) sts rem on each needle.

Now rep rnd 2 every rnd until 3 sts rem on each needle.

Cut yarn, leaving a 10"/25cm tail. Thread the needle with the tail and *insert through all sts, from 1st to last. Draw yarn back through all sts and tighten. Rep from * twice. Cut yarn, tie ends, and hide tails. (Figure 3)

Finishing

Make these socks as fancy as you like by adding crocheted edging, fringes, or both.

Fringes
Cut Yarn C into 10 (11, 12) 5"/13cm strands, so that each strand is thicker at the middle and thinner at the ends.

With RS facing and top of leg away from you, fold each strand in half and use hook to draw folded end downwards through every 4th st in rnd 29 (see figure 4, rightmost fringe). Pull the ends of the strand downwards and through the loop (see Figure 4, middle fringe). Pull to tighten (see Figure 4, leftmost fringe).

Crocheted rows
With RS facing, top of leg away from you, and Yarn D, insert hook under 1st CO st and *ch 2, sl st through next st. Rep from * around leg. Sl st through 1st ch. Cut yarn, tie ends, and hide tails.

With top of leg close to you, rep with Yarn E on rnds 7 and 19, inserting hook through each st of those rnds. Rep with Yarn F on rnd 13. (Figure 5)

Figure 4

Figure 5

This project was knit with

(A) 2 (2, 3) balls of Gedifra Fashion Trend, 51% wool/49% acrylic yarn, heavy worsted weight, 1¾oz/50g = approx 98yd/90m per ball, color #4504

(B) 1 ball of Gedifra Boheme, 43% merino wool/43% acrylic/14% polyamide yarn, bulky weight, 1¾oz/50g = approx 109yd/100m per ball, color #1825

(C) 1 ball of Gedifra Gigante, 100% wool yarn, super bulky weight, 1¾oz/50g = approx 33yd/30m per ball, color #2310

(D) 1 ball of Schachenmayr Hair, 65% mohair/35% acrylic yarn, Aran weight, 1¾oz/50g = approx 207yd/190m per ball, color #98

(E) 1 ball of Schachenmayr Hair, 65% mohair/35% acrylic yarn, Aran weight, 1¾oz/50g = approx 207yd/190m per ball, color #14

(F) 1 ball of Schachenmayr Hair, 65% mohair/35% acrylic yarn, Aran weight, 1¾oz/50g = approx 207yd/190m per ball, color #72

Dancing Queen Socks

These colorful socks are perfect for dancing, aerobics, or just jumping around. Make them particularly lively by adding a decorative Crocheted Flower (page 114).

EXPERIENCE LEVEL

■■□□ EASY

SIZES

Woman's small (woman's medium, woman's large)

LENGTH ON LEG

Above the ankle

MATERIALS AND TOOLS

Yarn A **4** MEDIUM : 147 (196, 245)yd/135 (180, 225)m of Medium weight yarn, cotton/acrylic, in variegated white, pink, and orange

Yarn B **3** LIGHT : 33yd/30m of Light weight yarn, cotton/acrylic, in orange
Knitting needles: Set of 5 dpn, 3 mm (size 3 U.S.) *or size to obtain gauge*
Crochet hook: 3.5 mm (E/4)
Scissors

GAUGE

12 sts and 18 rows = 2"/5cm with Yarn A in Stockinette Stitch
Always take time to check your gauge.

Instructions

NOTE: *Purl side is RS of this sock.*

LEG

With Yarn A, CO 40 (44, 48) sts.

Divide sts evenly between 4 needles—10 (11, 12) sts on each needle.

Work around in St st (k all sts) for 25 rnds, or desired length to beg of heel opening. End at Needle 3.

HEEL OPENING

Work around as follows:

Using spare needle, BO sts on Needle 4, then Needle 1—20 (22, 24) sts.

K all sts on Needles 2 and 3.

With spare needle, CO 28 (30, 32) sts.

K all sts on Needles 2 and 3.

Divide CO sts between Needles 4 and 1 as follows: Needle 4: K14 (15, 16); Needle 1: K14 (15, 16); Needles 2, 3: K all sts.

INSTEP

*Rnd 1: Needle 1: K to last 3 sts, skp, k1; Needles 2 and 3: K all sts; Needle 4: K1, k2tog, k to end.

Rnd 2: K all sts.

Rep from * four times, until there are 10 (11, 12) sts on Needles 1 and 4—40 (44, 48) sts total.

FOOT

Work around in k for 30 (36, 40) rnds, or desired length to toe opening. BO all sts.

Finishing

Crocheted leg edging

With RS facing, top of leg away from you, and Yarn B, insert hook under 1st CO st and ch 3, sl st into 2nd ch. *Sl st under next CO st, ch 2, sl st into 1st ch. Rep from * around top of sock. Sl st under 1st CO st. Cut yarn, tie ends, and hide tails.

Crocheted heel opening edging

With RS facing, top of leg away from you, and Yarn B, insert hook into right corner of rnd before heel opening. Ch 3, sl st into 2nd ch. *Sl st into 2nd st from hook, ch 2, sl st into 1st ch. Rep from * around heel opening. (Insert hook under CO sts until you reach left corner, then insert under BO sts.) Sl st into 1st corner st. Cut yarn, tie ends, and hide tails.

Crocheted toe opening edging

With RS facing, top of leg close to you, and Yarn B, insert hook under 1st BO st and ch 3, sl st into 2nd ch. *Sl st under next BO st, ch 2, sl st into 1st ch. Rep from * around toe opening. Sl st into 1st BO st. Cut yarn, tie ends, and hide tails.

This project was knit with

(A) 2 (2, 3) balls of Schachenmayr Punto, 55% cotton/45% acrylic yarn, Aran weight, 1¾oz/50g = approx 98yd/90m per ball, color #87

(B) 1 ball of Schachenmayr Jazz, 50% cotton/50% acrylic yarn, light weight, 1¾oz/50g = approx 137yd/125m per ball, color #29

The Truck Stops Here Socks

These socks are perfect for anyone with a love of trucks, buildings, and all other construction-related items. The project gives instructions for a different pattern for each sock, but you can make them identical if you prefer.

EXPERIENCE LEVEL

■■■□ INTERMEDIATE

SIZES

Woman's small/man's extra small (woman's medium/man's small, woman's large/man's medium)

LENGTH ON LEG

Lower calf

MATERIALS AND TOOLS

Yarn A (**6** SUPER BULKY): 164 (205, 246)yd/150 (188, 225)m of Super bulky weight yarn, wool/acrylic/polyamide, in dark blue

Yarn B (**6** SUPER BULKY): 38yd/35m of Super bulky weight yarn, wool/acrylic/polyamide, in army green

Yarn C (**5** BULKY): 27yd/25m of Bulky weight yarn, mohair/acrylic, in apricot

Yarn D (**5** BULKY): 27yd/25m of Bulky weight yarn, mohair/acrylic, in light yellow

Yarn E (**5** BULKY): 27yd/25m of Bulky weight yarn, mohair/acrylic, in light green

Knitting needles: Set of 5 dpn, 4 mm (size 6 U.S.) *or size to obtain gauge*

Crochet hook: 3.5 mm (E/4)

Scissors

Tapestry needle

3 round brown buttons, 1"/3cm in diameter

GAUGE

11 sts and 16 rows = 2"/5cm with Yarn A in Stockinette Stitch

10 sts and 16 rows = 2"/5cm with Yarn A in Rib Stitch

Always take time to check your gauge.

Instructions

TRUCK PATTERN

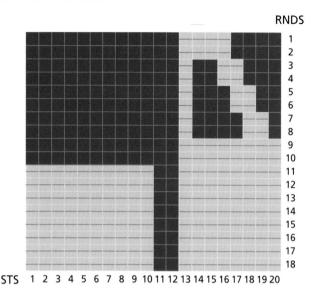

RNDS
1 2 3 4 5 6 7 8 9 10 11 12 13 14 15 16 17 18

STS 1 2 3 4 5 6 7 8 9 10 11 12 13 14 15 16 17 18 19 20

Truck Pattern Key
■ k1 st
▦ p1 st

BRICK PATTERN

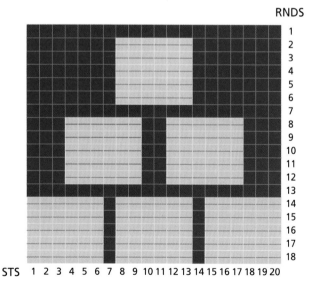

RNDS
1 2 3 4 5 6 7 8 9 10 11 12 13 14 15 16 17 18

STS 1 2 3 4 5 6 7 8 9 10 11 12 13 14 15 16 17 18 19 20

Brick Pattern Key
■ k1 st
▦ p1 st

CUFF

With Yarn B, CO 40 (44, 48) sts.

Divide sts evenly between 4 needles—10 (11, 12) sts on each needle.

Work around in k2, p2 rib for 1 rnd.

Join Yarn A. *With Yarn A, work around in k2, p2 rib for 2 rnds. With Yarn B, work around in k2, p2, rib for 2 rnds.

Rep from * twice. Cut Yarn B.

With Yarn A, work around in k2, p2 rib for 6 rnds.

LEG

Truck sock
With Yarn A, k all sts for 6 rnds, then work around in Truck Pattern. Pattern consists of 18 rnds and 20 sts. Needles 1 and 4: K all sts; Needles 2 and 3: Work in pattern.

Cont with Yarn A and k all sts for 12 rnds, or desired length to beg of heel. End at Needle 3.

Brick sock
With Yarn A, k all sts for 7 rnds, then work around in Brick Pattern. Pattern consists of 17 rnds and 20 sts. Needles 1 and 4: K all sts; Needles 2 and 3: Work in pattern.

Cont with Yarn A. K all sts for 12 rnds, or desired length to beg of heel. End at Needle 3.

HEEL FLAP

Start with Yarn B, and alternate with Yarn A every 3rd row.

Using spare needle, sl 1, k across sts from Needle 4, then Needle 1—19 (21, 23)sts; leave sts on Needles 2 and 3 unworked.

Work back and forth in St st (k1 row, p1 row) for 13 (15, 15) more rows.

....

HEEL

With Yarn A, work short rows as follows:
Sl 1, k12 (13, 14), skp, turn;
* sl 1, p6 (6, 6), p2tog, turn;
sl 1, k6 (6, 6), skp, turn.

Rep from * until all sts have been worked—8 (8, 8) sts on your needle.

Next row (RS): K4 (4, 4) sts onto Needle 4, then onto Needle 1.

....

GUSSET

Using Needle 1, pick up and k10 (11, 12) sts evenly spaced along edge of heel.

Cont to work-in-the-rnd and k sts on Needles 2 and 3.

Using spare needle, pick up and k10 (11, 12) sts evenly spaced along edge of heel, then k4 (4, 4) sts from Needle 4—14 (15, 16) sts on Needles 1 and 4.

....

INSTEP

*Rnd 1: Needle 1: K to last 3 sts, skp, k1; Needles 2 and 3: K all sts; Needle 4: K1, k2tog, k to end.

Rnd 2: K all sts.

Rep from * four times, until there are 10 (11, 12) sts on Needles 1 and 4—40 (44, 48) sts total.

FOOT

Work around in k for 28 (32, 36) rnds.

Join Yarn B and work around in k for 2 rounds.

....

TOE

Start with Yarn A, and alternate with Yarn B every 3rd rnd.

*Rnd 1: K all sts.

Rnd 2 (dec rnd): Needles 1 and 3: K to last 3 sts, skp, k1; Needles 2 and 4: K1, k2tog, k to end.

Rep from * until 7 (8, 8) sts rem on each needle.

Now rep rnd 2 every rnd until 3 sts rem on each needle.

Cut yarn, leaving a 10"/25cm tail. Thread the needle with Yarn A and *insert through all sts, from 1st to last. Draw yarn back through all sts and tighten. Rep from * twice. Cut yarn, tie ends, and hide tails.

....

Finishing

Crocheted truck

With RS facing, cuff close to you , and Yarn C, insert hook through bottom right p st of truck window. Ch 1, then sc 1 around concave area. Sl st under 1st ch. Cut yarn, tie ends, and hide tails.

With Yarn D, insert hook through bottom right p st of truck cab. Ch 1, then sc 1 all around the raised area. Sl st under 1st ch. Cut yarn, tie ends, and hide tails.

With Yarn E, insert hook through bottom right p st of truck bed. Ch 1, then sc 1 all around the raised area.

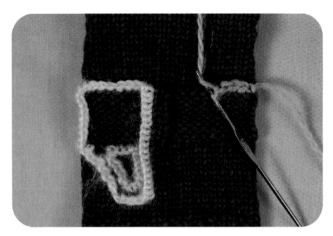

Figure 1

Figure 2

Figure 3

(Figure 1) Sl st under 1st ch. Cut yarn, tie ends, and hide tails.

With Yarn E, sew 2 buttons along the bottom of the truck bed, and 1 at the bottom of the truck cab. (Figure 2)

Crocheted bricks

With RS facing, cuff close to you, and Yarn C, insert hook through bottom right p st of top brick. Ch 1, then sc 1 all around the raised area. Sl st under 1st ch. Cut yarn.

With Yarn E, insert hook through bottom right p st of middle right brick. Ch 1, then sc 1 all around the raised area. Sl st under 1st ch. Rep around adjacent brick. Cut yarn.

With Yarn D, insert hook through bottom right p st of top right brick. Ch 1, then sc 1 all around the raised area. Sl st under 1st ch. Rep around adjacent bricks. Cut yarn, tie ends, and hide tails. (Figure 3)

This project was knit with

(A) 2 (3, 3) balls of Gedifra Shanina, 30% wool/30% acrylic/40% polyamide, super bulky weight, 1¾oz/50g = approx 82yd/75m per ball, color #5056

(B) 1 ball of Gedifra Shanina, 30% wool/30% acrylic/40% polyamide, super bulky weight, 1¾oz/50g = approx 82yd/75m per ball, color #5078

(C) 1 ball of Schachenmayr Mohana, 33% mohair/67% acrylic, chunky weight, 1¾oz/50g = approx 137yd/125m per ball, color #22

(D) 1 ball of Schachenmayr Mohana, 33% mohair/67% acrylic, chunky weight, 1¾oz/50g = approx 137yd/125m per ball, color #24

(E) 1 ball of Schachenmayr Mohana, 33% mohair/67% acrylic, chunky weight, 1¾oz/50g = approx 137yd/125m per ball, color #70

Super Shoesocks

Socks or shoes—can't decide which to wear? How about both! This pattern creates a comfortable sock with the fitted feel of a shoe. Laces add style and sensibility.

EXPERIENCE LEVEL

■■■□ INTERMEDIATE

SIZES

Woman's medium/man's small (woman's large/man's medium)

LENGTH ON LEG

Lower calf

MATERIALS AND TOOLS

Yarn A **BULKY 5** : 132 (198)yd/120 (180)m of Bulky weight yarn, acrylic/wool, in variegated olive, burgundy, blue, and brown

Yarn B **SUPER BULKY 6** : 82yd/75m of Super bulky weight yarn, wool/acrylic/polyamide, in army green
Knitting needles:
Pair of straight 4 mm (size 6 U.S.) *or size to obtain gauge*
Set of 5 dpn, 4 mm (size 6 U.S.) *or size to obtain gauge*
Crochet hook: 3.5 mm (E/4)
2 holders
Scissors
Tapestry needle
2 red/brown leather laces, 40"/1m long

GAUGE

10 sts and 12 rows = 2"/5cm with Yarn A in Stockinette Stitch
9 sts and 12 rows = 2"/5cm with Yarn A in Rib Stitch
Always take time to check your gauge.

Instructions

Figure 1

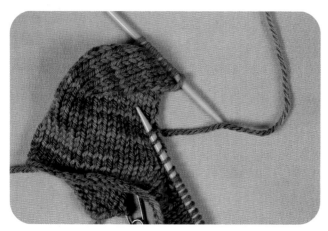

Figure 2

CUFF

With Yarn A and straight needles, CO 38 (46) sts.

Work in k2, p2 rib for 1 row. K the knits and p the purls for 25 more rows.

LEG

Work in St st (k1 row, p1 row) for 4 rows.

HEEL FLAP

Move 1st and last 9 (11) sts onto holders and leave unworked.

With 20 (24) sts on your needle, cont in St st (k1 row, p1 row) for 14 (16) more rows.

HEEL

Work short rows as follows:
Sl 1, k12 (14), skp, turn;
*sl 1, p6 , p2tog, turn;
sl 1, k6 , skp, turn.

Rep from * until all sts have been worked—8 sts on your needle. Cut yarn. (Figure 1)

Next row (WS): With Yarn A and regular needles, k 1st 9 (11) sts from holder.

Using same needle (your working needle), pick up and k10 (12) sts evenly spaced along edge of heel. (Figure 2)

Using working needle, k8 sts from the other needle and pick up and k10 (12) sts evenly spaced along edge of heel. K last 9 (11) sts from holder. There are now 46 (54) sts on your needle.

Next row (RS): P all sts.

INSTEP

*Row 1 (dec row): K10 (12) sts, k2 tog, k to last 12 (24) sts, skp, k10 (12) sts.

Row 2: P all sts.

Rep from * four times, until there are 38 (46) sts on your needle.

FOOT

Row 1 (inc row): CO 1 st, k all sts, CO 1 st—40 (48) sts total.

Now we start working in the round. Divide sts evenly between 4 dpn—10 (12) sts on each needle.

Work around in St st (k all sts) for 25 (30) rnds, or desired length to beg of toe.

TOE

*Rnd 1: K all sts.

Rnd 2 (dec rnd): Needles 1 and 3: K to last 3 st, skp, k1; Needles 2 and 4: K1, k2tog, k to end.

Rep from * until 6 (7) sts rem on each needle.

Now rep rnd 2 every rnd until 3 sts rem on each needle.

Cut yarn, leaving a 10"/25cm tail. Thread the needle with the tail and *insert through all sts, from 1st to last. Draw yarn back through all sts and tighten. Rep from * twice. Cut yarn, tie ends, and hide tails.

Finishing

CROCHETED EDGING

With RS facing, cuff away from you, and Yarn B, insert hook in corner st on left side of sock opening. Ch 3, hdc 1 into same st, *sc 1 in 3rd st from hook, ch 2, hdc 1 into same st. Rep from * twelve times down left side of sock opening. At center of sock opening, sc 1 in 4 following sts. Sc 1 in next st, ch 2, hdc 1 in the same st, then rep from * up right side of sock opening, and around top of sock. End with sl st into 2nd ch from beg. Cut yarn, tie ends, and hide tails.

NOTE: *Pattern should be reped exactly on each side of sock opening to form 13 eyelets on either side.*

TONGUE

With WS facing, cuff away from you, and sock opening up, find center of sock at 6th rnd from sock opening on top of foot. Count 5 sts to the right of center, and 5 sts to the left. With knitting needle, pick up these 10 center sts. Join Yarn A and k all sts for 48 rows (Figure 3).

Row 49 (inc row): K2, k1inc1, k4, k1inc1, k to end. There are now 12 sts on your needle.

Figure 3

Row 50: K all sts.

Rows 51–52: BO 3, k to end.

Row 53: BO rem 6 sts.

Connecting tongue and sock

With RS facing, cuff away from you, and sock opening up, find 6th rnd from sock opening on top of foot, and count 4 sts to the right of center. With Yarn B, insert hook into 4th k st to right of center in sock, then into 1st k st of 1st row of tongue. Sl st into every 4th st from center and 1st st of tongue in every row to the top of the sock, to make a seam that is parallel to sock opening along right side (Figure 4). Cut yarn, tie ends, and hide tails.

Find 6th rnd from sock opening on top of foot and count 4 sts to the left of center. Rep as on right side to make identical parallel seam on the left.

Tongue edging

With Yarn B, insert hook into 1st k st in the loose area of the shoe tongue and ch 3, then hdc 1 into same st. *Sc in 3rd st from hook, ch 2, hdc 1 into same st. Rep from * around top of tongue until you reach the other corner. Cut yarn, tie ends, and hide tails.

Lacing

Lace the shoe in a traditional crisscross pattern, or any other manner you like. (Figure 5)

This project was knit with

(A) 2 (3) balls of Schachenmayr Joana, 50% acrylic/50% new cool wool, chunky weight, 1¾oz/50g = approx 66yd/60m per ball, color #83

(B) 1 ball of Gedifra Shanina, 30% wool/30% acrylic/40% polyamide, super bulky weight, 1¾oz/50g = approx 82yd/75m per ball, color #5078

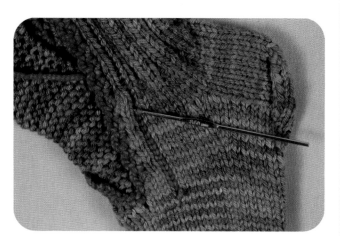

Figure 4

Figure 5

Zingy Zigzag Socks

This traditional sock pattern gets an untraditional look thanks to the use of a colorful yarn. Add the Lucky Leather Sock Pocket (page 116) for a pair of socks that includes an unusual accessory.

EXPERIENCE LEVEL

■■□□ EASY

SIZES

Woman's large/man's medium (woman's extra large/man's large)

LENGTH ON LEG

Mid-calf

MATERIALS AND TOOLS

BULKY 5 264yd/240m of Bulky weight yarn, acrylic/wool, in variegated green, pink, and gray
Knitting needles: Set of 5 dpn, 4 mm (size 6 U.S.) *or size to obtain gauge*
Scissors
Tapestry needle

GAUGE

11 sts and 14 rows = 2"/5cm in Stockinette Stitch
11 sts and 14 rows = 2"/5cm in 5 x 1 Rib Stitch
11 sts and 14 rows = 2"/5cm in 6 x 1 Rib Stitch
12 sts and 14 rows = 2"/5cm in 2 x 2 Rib Stitch
Always take time to check your gauge.

Instructions

CUFF
CO 48 (56) sts.

Divide sts evenly between 4 needles—12 (14) sts on each needle.

Work around in k2, p2 rib for 18 (22) rnds, or any desired length.

LEG
Cont to work in k5, p1 (k6, p1) rib for 20 (25) rnds, or desired length to beg of heel flap. End at Needle 3.

HEEL FLAP

NOTE: *Purl side is RS of the gusset.*

Using spare needle, sl 1, p across sts from Needle 4, then Needle 1—23 (27) sts; leave sts on Needles 2, 3 unworked.

Work back and forth in St st (k1 row, p1 row) for 15 (17) more rows. End with a WS row.

HEEL

Work short rows as follows:
Sl 1, p14 (18), p2tog, turn;
*sl 1, k6 (8), skp, turn;
sl 1, p6 (8), p2tog, turn.

Rep from * until all sts have been worked—8 (10) sts on your needle.

Next row (RS): K4 (5) sts onto Needle 4, then k4 (5) sts onto Needle 1.

GUSSET

Using Needle 1, pick up and k11 (12) sts evenly spaced along edge of heel.

Work around in k5, p1 (k6, p1) rib on Needles 2 and 3.

Using spare needle, pick up and k11 (12) sts evenly spaced along edge of heel, then k4 (5) sts from Needle 4—15 (17) sts on Needles 1 and 4.

INSTEP

*Rnd 1: Needle 1: K to last 3 sts, skp, k1; Needles 2 and 3: K5, p1 (k6, p1); Needle 4: K1, k2tog, k to end.

Rnd 2: Needles 1 and 4: K all sts; Needles 2 and 3: K5, p1 (k6, p1) rib.

Rep from * three times, until 12 (14) sts rem on each needle.

FOOT

Work around as follows:

Needles 1 and 4: K all sts; Needles 2 and 3: K5, p1 (k6, p1) rib for 35 (40) rounds, or desired length to beg of toe.

TOE

Rnd 1: K all sts.
Rnd 2: P all sts.
*Rnd 3: K all sts.
Rnd 4 (dec rnd): Needles 1 and 3: K to last 3 sts, skp, k1; Needles 2 and 4: K1, k2tog, k to end.
Rep from * until 10 (12) sts rem on each needle.

Now rep rnd 4 every rnd until 3 sts rem on each needle.

Cut yarn, leaving a 10"/25cm tail. Thread the needle with the tail and *insert through all sts, from 1st to last. Draw yarn back through all sts and tighten. Rep from * twice. Cut yarn, tie ends, and hide tails.

This project was knit with

4 balls of Schachenmayr Joana, 50% acrylic/50% new cool wool, chunky weight, 1¾oz/50g = approx 66yd/60m per ball, color #82

Diamond Delight

The elegant diamond pattern on these socks is knit along the leg and the top of the foot. The bottom of the foot is knit in Stockinette Stitch, which is more comfortable for walking on.

EXPERIENCE LEVEL

■■■▶ EXPERIENCED

SIZES

Woman's small/medium

LENGTH ON LEG

Lower calf (cuff unfolded); above the ankle (cuff folded)

MATERIALS AND TOOLS

Yarn A **4** : 328yd/300m of Medium weight yarn, nylon/acrylic/kid mohair, in coral

Yarn B **4** : 328yd/300m of Medium weight yarn, nylon/acrylic/kid mohair, in apricot

Yarn C **4** : 306yd/280m of Medium weight yarn, cotton/extra fine merino, in peach

Knitting needles: Set of 5 dpn, 3 mm (size 3 U.S.) *or size to obtain gauge*

Scissors

Tapestry needle

GAUGE

12 sts and 18 rows = 2"/5cm with Yarn C in Stockinette Stitch

13 sts and 14 rows = 2"/5cm with Yarn A and B in Rib Stitch

18 sts and 32 rows = 3"/8cm with Yarn C in Diamond Pattern

Always take time to check your gauge.

Instructions

Figure 1

DIAMOND PATTERN

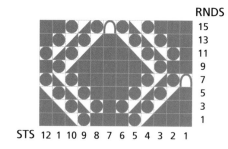

Diamond Pattern Key

■ - K1

● - YO

◢ - K2tog

◣ - SKPO

∩ - Double Left-Slanting Decrease

CUFF

With Yarn A and B tog, CO 48 sts.

Divide sts evenly between 4 needles—12 sts on each needle.

Work around in k1, p1 rib for 20 rnds, or desired length to beg of leg.

LEG

Join Yarn C and work around in Diamond Pattern. Pattern consists of 16 rnds and 12 sts.
K every 2nd rnd. Rep pattern twice for 32 rnds in total on each needle. (Figure 1)

HEEL FLAP

Join Yarn A and B tog, and using spare needle, sl 1, k across sts from Needle 4, then Needle 1—24 sts; leave sts on Needles 2 and 3 unworked.

Work back and forth in St st (k1 row, p1 row) for 13 more rows. End with WS row.

HEEL

Work short rows as follows:
Sl 1, k14, skp, turn;
*sl 1, p6 p2tog, turn;
sl 1, k6, skp, turn.
Rep from * until all sts have been worked—8 sts on your needle.
Next row (RS): With Yarn C, k4 sts onto Needle 4, then onto Needle 1.

GUSSET

Using Needle 1, pick up and k11 sts evenly spaced along edge of heel.

Cont to work in-the-rnd and work in pattern on Needles 2 and 3 (beg pattern from 1st rnd).

Using spare needle, pick up and k11 sts evenly spaced along edge of heel, then k4 sts from Needle 4—15 sts on Needles 1 and 4.

INSTEP
*Rnd 1: K all sts.

Rnd 2: Needle 1: K to last 3 sts, skp, k1; Needles 2 and 3: Work in pattern; Needle 4: K1, k2tog, k to end.

Rep from * three times, until 12 sts rem on each needle—48 sts total.

FOOT
Work around as follows for 31 rnds, or desired length to beg of toe:
Needles 1 and 4: K all sts; Needles 2 and 3: Work in pattern.

Work around in k for 2 more rnds.

TOE
*Rnd 1: K all sts.

Rnd 2 (dec rnd): Needles 1 and 3: K to last 3 sts, skp, k;
Needles 2 and 4: K1, k2tog, k to end.

Rep from * until 8 sts rem on each needle.
Now rep rnd 2 every rnd until 3 sts rem on each needle.

Cut yarn, leaving a 10"/25cm tail. Thread the needle with the tail and *insert through all sts, from 1st to last. Draw yarn back through all sts and tighten. Rep from * twice.
Cut yarn, tie ends, and hide tails.

This project was knit with

(A) 1 ball of Schachenmayr Kid Light, 35% nylon/35% acrylic/30% kid mohair, Aran weight, 1¾oz/50g = approx 328yd/300m per ball, color #34
(B) 1 ball of Schachenmayr Kid Light, 35% nylon/35% acrylic/30% kid mohair, Aran weight, 1¾oz/50g = approx 328yd/300m per ball, color #27
(C) 2 balls of Gedifra Airmix, 30% cotton/62% extra fine merino/8% polyamide, Aran weight, 1¾oz/50g = approx 153yd/140m per ball, color #7020

Wonderland of Wool Socks

This pattern features a violet and silver design similar to the patterns developed in Fair Isle, a small island in northern Scotland famous for its colorful knits. These socks also feature a lovely fluffy edging.

EXPERIENCE LEVEL

■■■□ EXPERIENCED

SIZES

Woman's small/medium

LENGTH ON LEG

Lower calf

MATERIALS AND TOOLS

Yarn A (4 MEDIUM): 306yd/280m of Medium weight yarn, cotton/extra fine merino/polyamide, in sky blue

Yarn B (4 MEDIUM): 328yd/300m of Medium weight yarn, nylon/acrylic/kid mohair, in light blue

Yarn C (4 MEDIUM): 27yd/25m of Medium weight yarn, viscose/metallic polyester, in yellow gold

Yarn D (4 MEDIUM): 153yd/140m of Medium weight yarn, cotton/extra fine merino/polyamide, in violet
Knitting needles: Set of 5 dpn, 3 mm (size 3 U.S.) *or size to obtain gauge*
Crochet hook: 3.5 mm (E/4)
Scissors
Tapestry needle

GAUGE

12 sts and 18 rows = 2"/5cm with Yarn A in Stockinette Stitch
12 sts and 18 rows = 2"/5cm with Yarn A in Rib Stitch
Always take time to check your gauge.

Instructions

FAIR ISLE PATTERN

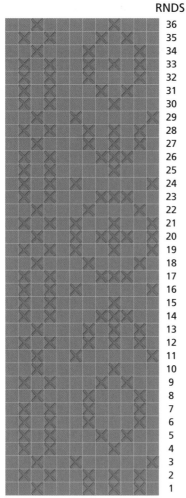

RNDS 36–1

STS 12 11 10 9 8 7 6 5 4 3 2 1

Fair Isle Pattern Key

 - MC is Yarn A

✕ - CC is Yarn D

TOE TOP PATTERN

RNDS 3 2 1

STS 2 1

Toe Top Pattern Key

◼ - MC is Yarn A

✕ - CC is Yarn D

CUFF

With Yarn A, CO 48 sts.

Divide sts between 4 needles—12 sts on each needle.

Work around in k for 1 rnd.

Join Yarns B and C tog, and work around in k for 2 rnds.

With Yarn A, work around in k for 2 rnds.

Work around in k2, p2 rib for 6 rnds.

Work around in k for 2 rnds.

Join Yarns B and C tog, and work around in k for 2 rnds.

LEG

With Yarn A, k all sts for 2 rnds. Work around in k following Fair Isle Pattern on each needle for 36 rnds. Pattern consists of 36 rnds and 12 sts.

Cont with Yarn A, k all sts for 2 rnds, or desired length to beg of heel flap. End at Needle 3.

HEEL FLAP

Join Yarns B and C tog. Using spare needle, sl 1, k across sts from Needle 4, then Needle 1—23 sts; leave sts on Needles 2 and 3 unworked.

Work back and forth in St st (k1 row, p1 row) for 1 row.

Join Yarn A, and cont with St st for 14 more rows. End with a WS row.

HEEL

Work short rows as follows:

Sl 1, k14, skp, turn;

*sl 1, p6, p2tog, turn;

sl 1, k6, skp, turn.

Rep from * until all sts have been worked—8 sts on your needle.

Next row (RS): With Yarn B and C tog, k4 sts onto Needle 4, then onto Needle 1.

GUSSET

Using Needle 1, pick up and k12 sts evenly spaced along edge of heel.

Cont to work in-the-rnd and k sts on Needles 2 and 3.

Using spare needle, pick up and k12 sts evenly spaced along edge of heel, then k4 sts from Needle 4—16 sts on Needles 1 and 4.

Work around in k for 1 rnd.

INSTEP

With Yarn A,

*Rnd 1: K all sts.

Rnd 2: Needle 1: K to last 3 sts, skp, k1; Needles 2 and 3: K all sts; Needle 4: K1, k2tog, k to end.

Rep from * four times, until 12 sts rem on each needle—48 sts total.

FOOT

Work around in k for 26 rnds, or desired length to beg of toe.

Join Yarns B and C tog, and work around in k for 2 rnds.

With Yarn A, work around in k for 1 rnd, then work around in k following Toe Top Pattern for 3 rnds. Pattern consists of 3 rnds and 2 sts. Rep pattern six times on each needle.

With Yarn A, work around in k for 1 rnd.

Join Yarn B and C tog, and work around in k for 2 rnds.

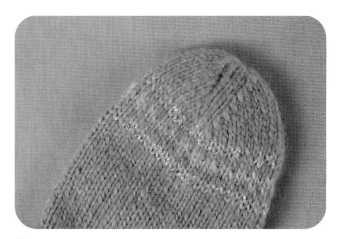

Figure 1

Figure 2

TOE

With Yarn A,

*Rnd 1: K all sts.

Rnd 2 (dec rnd): Needles 1 and 3: K to last 3 sts, skp, k1; Needles 2 and 4: K1, k2tog, k to end.

Rep from * until 7 sts rem on each needle.

Now rep rnd 2 every rnd until 3 sts rem on each needle.

Cut yarn, leaving a 10"/25cm tail. Thread the needle with the tail and *insert through all sts, from 1st to last. Draw yarn back through all sts and tighten. Rep from * twice. Cut yarn, tie ends, and hide tails. (Figure 1)

Finishing

CROCHETED EDGING

With RS facing, top of cuff away from you, and Yarn B, insert hook under 1st CO st and ch 3, dc 1 under same st, ch 2, dc 2 under same st.

*Dc 2 under 2nd CO st from hook, ch 2, dc 2 under same st. Rep from * all around top of sock. Sl st in 3rd ch from beg. Cut yarn, tie ends, and hide tails. (Figure 2)

This project was knit with

(A) 2 balls of Gedifra Airmix, 30% cotton/62% extra fine merino/8% polyamide, Aran weight, 1¾oz/50g = approx 153yd/140m per ball, color #7080

(B) 1 ball of Schachenmayr Kid Light, 35% nylon/35% acrylic/30% kid mohair, Aran weight, 1¾oz/50g = approx 328yd/300m per ball, color #65

(C) 1 ball of Anchor Arista, 80% viscose/20% metallic polyester, Aran weight, ¾ oz/25g = approx 109yd/100m per ball, color #300

(D) 1 ball of Gedifra Airmix, 30% cotton/62% extra fine merino/8% polyamide, Aran weight, 1¾oz/50g = approx 153yd/140m per ball, color #7037

Traditionally Cable Socks

Cable socks are a sock drawer staple. No winter wardrobe is complete without at least one pair to wear with your warmest winter boots. Use a solid-color yarn for a staid pair of socks, or multicolored yarn for something a little funkier.

EXPERIENCE LEVEL

■■■□ INTERMEDIATE

SIZES

Woman's small/medium (man's medium/large)

LENGTH ON LEG

Mid-calf (cuff unfolded); lower calf (cuff folded)

MATERIALS AND TOOLS

Yarn A **BULKY 5** : 548yd/500m of Bulky weight, mohair/acrylic, in variegated burgundy, brown, blue, and orange

Yarn B **BULKY 5** : 274yd/250m of Bulky weight, mohair/acrylic, in apricot
Knitting needles: Set of 5 dpn, 4 mm (size 6 U.S.) *or size to obtain gauge*
Cable needle, 4 mm (size 6 U.S.) *or size to obtain gauge*
Scissors
Tapestry needle

GAUGE

10 sts and 12 rows = 2"/5cm with Yarn A and B in Stockinette Stitch
10 sts and 12 rows = 2"/5cm with 2 strands of Yarn A in 2 x 2 Rib Stitch
10 sts and 12 rows = 2"/5cm with 2 strands of Yarn A in 3 x 3 Rib Stitch
10 sts and 12 rows = 2"/5cm with Yarn A and B in Cable Pattern
Always take time to check your gauge.

Instructions

CABLE TWIST

Figure 1

Figure 2

Yarn in photos is Schachenmayr Boston, in burgundy, for better visibility in sample photos

CUFF

With 2 strands of Yarn A, CO 40 (48) sts.

Divide sts evenly between 4 needles—10 (12) sts on each needle.

Work around in k2, p2 (k3, p3) rib for 12 rnds, or desired length to beg of leg.

LEG

With Yarn A and Yarn B tog, work around in Cable Pattern as follows:

*Rnds 1–9: P2, k6, p2 (p3, k6, p3).

Rnd 10 (cable twist): P2 (3), sl next 3 sts onto cable needle, hold in front (or back) of work (Figure 1), k next 3 sts, k3 sts from cable needle (Figure 2), p2 (3).

Rep from * three times.

Rnds 31--36: Work as for rnds 1–6. End at Needle 3.

HEEL FLAP

With 2 strands of Yarn A and using spare needle, sl 1, k across sts from Needle 4, then Needle 1—19 (23) sts; leave sts on Needles 2 and 3 unworked.

Work back and forth in St st (k1 row, p1 row) for 13 (15) rows. End with WS row.

HEEL

Work short rows as follows:
Sl 1, k12 (14), skp, turn;
*sl 1, p6 (6), p2tog, turn;
sl 1, k6 (6), skp, turn.

Rep from * until all sts have been worked—8 (8) sts on your needle.

With Yarn A and B tog, k4 sts onto Needle 4, then onto Needle 1.

GUSSET

Using Needle 1, pick up and k10 (12) sts evenly spaced along edge of heel.

Cont to work in-the-rnd and k sts on Needles 2 and 3.

Using spare needle, pick up and k10 (12) sts evenly spaced along edge of heel, then k4 sts from Needle 4—14 (16) sts on Needles 1 and 4.

INSTEP

*Rnd 1: Needles 1 and 4: K all sts; Needles 2 and 3: Work in Cable Pattern (cont pattern from 6th rnd).

Rnd 2: Needle 1: K to last 3 sts, skp, k1; Needles 2 and 3: Cont to work in pattern; Needle 4: K1, k2tog, k to end.

Rep from * four times, until 10 (12) sts rem on each needle—40 (48) sts total.

NOTE: *Remember to twist every 10th round, beginning from start of Cable Pattern in leg. Since round 1 of the instep is round 36 from beginning of pattern, you'll make the 1st twist of the instep on round 5.*

FOOT

Work around as follows for 24 (36) rnds, or desired length to beg of toe:

Needles 1 and 4: K all sts; Needles 2 and 3: Work in Cable Pattern (cont pattern from 4th rnd).

TOE

With 2 strands of Yarn A,

*Rnd 1: K all sts.

Rnd 2 (dec rnd): Needles 1 and 3: K to last 3 sts, skp, k1; Needles 2 and 4: K1, k2tog, k to end.

Rep from * until 7 (8) sts rem on each needle.

Now rep rnd 2 every rnd until 3 sts rem on each needle.

Cut yarn, leaving a 10"/25cm tail. Thread the needle with the tail and *insert through all sts, from 1st to last. Draw yarn back through all sts and tighten. Rep from * twice. Cut yarn, tie ends, and hide tails. (Figure 3)

This project was knit with

(A) 4 balls of Schachenmayr Mohana Color, 33% mohair/67% acrylic, chunky weight, 1¾oz/50g = approx 137yd/125m per ball, color #86
(B) 2 balls of Schachenmayr Mohana, 33% mohair/67% acrylic, chunky weight, 1¾oz/50g = approx 137yd/125m per ball, color #24

Figure 3

Summer Net Socks

These socks are cool, comfortable, and elegant. You'll need a dainty string or ribbon to tie them onto your ankle—the Hemp Leaf Ribbon (page 118) is perfect.

EXPERIENCE LEVEL

■■■□ INTERMEDIATE

SIZES

Woman's small (woman's medium)

LENGTH ON LEG

Below the ankle

MATERIALS AND TOOLS

LIGHT 3 218yd/200m of Light weight yarn, cotton, in variegated peach, olive, and beige
Knitting needles: Set of 5 dpn, 3 mm (size 3 U.S.) *or size to obtain gauge*
Crochet hook: 3.5 mm (E/4)
Scissors
Tapestry needle

GAUGE

14 sts and 18 rows = 2"/5cm in Stockinette Stitch
14 sts and 18 rows = 2"/5cm in Net Pattern
Always take time to check your gauge.

Instructions

NET PATTERN

RNDS
3
1

STS 4 3 2 1

Net Pattern Key

■ - K1

● - YO

∩ - Double Left-Slanting Decrease

LEG

CO 48 sts.

Divide sts evenly between 4 needles—12 sts on each needle.

Work around in k for 2 rnds, then work around in Net Pattern for 12 rnds. Pattern consists of 4 rnds and 4 sts. K every 2nd rnd. Rep pattern three times on each needle.

HEEL FLAP

Using spare needle, sl 1, k across sts from Needle 4, then Needle 1—23 sts; leave sts on Needles 2 and 3 unworked.

Work back and forth in St st (k1 row, p1 row) for 15 (17) more rows. End with WS row.

HEEL

Work short rows as follows:
Sl 1, k14, skp, turn;
*sl 1, p6, p2tog, turn;
sl 1, k6, skp, turn.

Rep from * until all sts have been worked—8 sts on your needle.

Next row (RS): K4 sts onto Needle 4, then onto Needle 1.

GUSSET

Using Needle 1, pick up and k12 (14) sts evenly spaced along edge of heel.

Cont to work in-the-rnd and work in pattern on Needles 2 and 3 (beg pattern from 1st rnd).

Using spare needle, pick up and k12 (14) sts evenly spaced along edge of heel, then k4 sts from Needle 4—16 (18) sts on Needles 1 and 4.

INSTEP

*Rnd 1: K all sts.

Rnd 2: Needle 1: K to last 3 sts, skp, k1; Needles 2 and 3: Work in pattern (cont pattern from 3rd rnd); Needle 4: K1, k2tog, k to end.

Rep from * four (six) times, until 12 sts rem on each needle.

FOOT

Work around in k for 1 rnd.

Needles 1 and 4: K all sts; Needles 2 and 3: Work in pattern (cont pattern from 3rd rnd) for 32 (40) rnds, or desired length to beg of toe. (Figure 1)

TOE

*Rnd 1: K all sts.

Rnd 2 (dec rnd): Needles 1 and 3: K to last 3 sts, skp, k1; Needles 2 and 4: K1, k2tog, k to end.

Rep from * until 7 sts rem on each needle.

Now rep rnd 2 every rnd until 3 sts rem on each needle.

Cut yarn, leaving a 10"/25cm tail. Thread the needle with the tail and *insert through all sts, from 1st to last. Draw yarn back through all sts and tighten. Rep from * twice. Cut yarn and hide tails.

Finishing

CROCHETED EDGING

NOTE: *This edging creates the loops that are used to support the Hemp Leaf Ribbon (page 118). It can be added to any sock to provide a base for supporting a string or ribbon.*

With RS facing and toe close to you, insert hook under 1st CO st and *ch 4, sl st under 2nd CO st from hook. Rep from * all around top of sock. Cut yarn, tie ends, and hide tails.

This project was knit with

2 balls of Gedifra Frisetto Color, worsted weight, 100% cotton, 1¾oz/50g = approx 109yd/100m per ball, color #8802

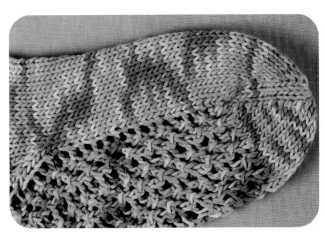

Figure 1

Wavy Sea Socks

These fuzzy white socks are perfect for keeping sea-lovers at ease when on land. Adding Pompon on a String (page 120) completes the look.

EXPERIENCE LEVEL

■■■☐ INTERMEDIATE

SIZES

Woman's small (woman's medium)

LENGTH ON LEG

Lower calf

MATERIALS AND TOOLS

BULKY
Yarn A **5** : 274yd/250m of Bulky weight yarn, mohair/acrylic, in white

SUPER BULKY
Yarn B **6** : 109yd/100m of Super bulky weight yarn, merino wool/acrylic/polyamide, in navy

Knitting needles: Set of 5 dpn, 3 mm (size 3 U.S.) *or size to obtain gauge*
Crochet hook: 3.5 mm (E/4)
Scissors
Tapestry needle

GAUGE

13 sts and 15 rows = 2"/5cm with Yarn A in Stockinette Stitch
12 sts and 15 rows = 2"/5cm with Yarn A in Rib Stitch
Always take time to check your gauge.

Instructions

WAVE PATTERN

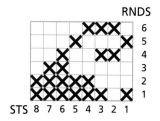

LEFT SOCK

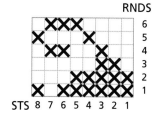

RIGHT SOCK

Wave Pattern Key
☐ - MC is Yarn A
✗ - CC is Yarn B

CUFF

With Yarn A, CO 40 (48) sts.

Divide sts between 4 needles—10 (12) sts on each needle.

Work around in k2, p2 rib for 12 rnds, or desired length to beg of leg.

LEG

Work in St st (k all sts) for 3 rnds.

Join Yarn B and work around in k following Wave Pattern for 6 rnds. Pattern consists of 6 rnds and 8 sts. Work in pattern on each needle. Start pattern again on rem sts on each needle and cont pattern on next needle.

NOTE: *The finished sock will have 5 (6) complete waves.*

With Yarn A, work in St st (k all sts) for 24 more rnds, or desired length to beg of heel flap. End at Needle 3.

HEEL FLAP

Using spare needle, sl 1, k across sts from Needle 4, then Needle 1—19 (23) sts; leave sts on Needles 2 and 3 unworked.

Work back and forth in St st (k1 row, p1 row) for 13 (15) more rows. End with WS row.

HEEL

Work short rows as follows:
Sl 1, k12 (14), skp, turn;
*sl 1, p6 (6), p2tog, turn;
sl 1, k6 (6) skp, turn.

Rep from * until all sts have been worked—8 (8) sts on your needle.

Next row (RS): K4 (4) sts onto Needle 4, then k4 (4) onto Needle 1.

GUSSET

Using Needle 1, pick up and k10 (12) sts evenly spaced along edge of heel.

Cont to work in-the-rnd and k sts on Needles 2 and 3.

Using spare needle, pick up and k10 (12) sts evenly spaced along edge of heel, then k4 (4) sts from Needle 4—14 (16) sts on Needles 1 and 4.

INSTEP

*Rnd 1: K all sts

Rnd 2: Needle 1: K to last 3 sts, skp, k1; Needles 2 and 3: K all sts; Needle 4: K1, k2tog, k to end.

Rep from * four times, until 10 (12) sts rem on Needles 1 and 4—40 (48) sts total.

FOOT

Work around in k for 30 (36) rnds, or desired length to beg of toe.

TOE

*Rnd 1: K all sts.

Rnd 2 (dec rnd): Needles 1 and 3: K to last 3 sts, skp, k1; Needles 2 and 4: K1, k2tog, k to end.

Rep from * until 6 (7) sts rem on each needle.

Now rep rnd 2 every rnd until 3 sts rem on each needle.

Cut yarn, leaving a 10"/25cm tail. Thread the needle with the tail and *insert through all sts, from 1st to last. Draw yarn back through all sts and tighten. Rep from * twice. Cut yarn, tie ends, and hide tails.

This project was knit with

(A) 2 balls of Schachenmayr Mohana, 33% mohair/67% acrylic, chunky weight, 1¾oz/50g = approx 137yd/125m per ball, color #01

(B) 1 ball of Gedifra Boheme, 43% merino wool/43% acrylic/14% polyamide yarn, bulky weight, 1¾oz/50g = approx 109yd/100m per ball, color #1868

Cute as a Bunny Cuffed Socks

These cuffed socks are perfect for keeping your feet and ankles warm. By adding a pair of Funny Bunnies (page 122) you'll ensure that your ankles are never lonely again!

EXPERIENCE LEVEL

■■□□ EASY

SIZES

Woman's small/medium (woman's large)

LENGTH ON LEG

Lower calf (cuff unfolded); above the ankle (cuff folded)

MATERIALS AND TOOLS

Yarn A **BULKY 5** : 175yd/160m of Bulky weight yarn, wool/nylon/acrylic, in variegated brown, blue, and white

Yarn B **BULKY 5** : 137yd/125m of Bulky weight yarn, mohair/acrylic, in apricot
Knitting needles: Set of 5 dpn, 4 mm (size 6 U.S.) *or size to obtain gauge*
Crochet hook: 3.5 mm (E/4)
Scissors
Tapestry needle

GAUGE

10 sts and 15 rows = 2"/5cm with Yarn A in Stockinette Stitch
10 sts and 15 rows = 2"/5cm with Yarn A in Rib Stitch
Always take time to check your gauge.

Instructions

CUFF

With Yarn A and knitting needles, CO 40 (48) sts.

Work in k2, p2 rib for 1 rnd. K the knits and p the purls for 15 (17) more rows.

Divide sts evenly between 4 needles—10 (12) sts on each needle.

Work around in k2, p2 rib for 18 (20) rnds.

LEG

Work around in St st (k all sts) for 8 (10) rnds, or desired length to beg of heel flap. End at Needle 3.

HEEL FLAP

Using spare needle, sl 1, k across sts from Needle 4, then Needle 1—19 (23) sts; leave sts on Needles 2 and 3 unworked.

Work back and forth in St st (k1 row, p1 row) for 15 (17) more rows. End with WS row.

HEEL

Work short rows as follows:
Sl 1, k12 (14), skp, turn;
*sl 1, p6 (6), p2tog, turn;
sl 1, k6 (6), skp, turn.

Rep from * until all sts have been worked—8 (8) sts on your needle.

Next row (RS): K4 (4) sts onto Needle 4, then k4 (4) sts onto Needle 1.

GUSSET

Using Needle 1, pick up and k10 (12) sts evenly spaced along edge of heel.

Cont to work in-the-rnd and k sts on Needles 2 and 3.

Using spare needle, pick up and k10 (12) sts evenly spaced along edge of heel, then k4 (4) sts from Needle 4—14 (16) sts on Needles 1 and 4.

INSTEP

*Rnd 1: K all sts.

Rnd 2: Needle 1: K to last 3 sts, skp, k1; Needles 2 and 3: K all sts; Needle 4: K1, k2tog, k to end.

Rep from * four times, until 10 (12) sts rem on each needle—40 (48) sts total.

FOOT

Work around in k for 24 (30) rnds, or desired length to beg of toe.

TOE

*Rnd 1: K all sts.

Rnd 2 (dec rnd): Needles 1 and 3: K to last 3 sts, skp, k1; Needles 2 and 4: K1, k2tog, k to end.

Rep from * until 5 (6) sts rem on each needle.

Now rep rnd 2 every rnd until 3 sts rem on each needle.

Cut yarn, leaving a 10"/25cm tail. Thread the needle with the tail and *insert through all sts, from 1st to last. Draw yarn back through all sts and tighten. Rep from * twice. Cut yarn, tie ends, and hide tails.

Finishing

Crochet edging
With WS facing, cuff away from you, and Yarn B,

Rnd 1: Insert hook under 1st CO st and ch 3, then hdc 1 under 2nd CO st from hook. *Ch 1, hdc 1 under 2nd st from hook. Rep from * around the top of sock until last CO st. Cont down right side and up left side of cuff opening. End with sl st into 2nd ch from beg.

Rnd 2: Ch 1, sc 1 under ch of prev rnd, sc 1 into hdc of prev rnd. *Sc 1 under ch, sc 1 into hdc. Rep from * around top of sock and cuff opening. End with sl st into 1st ch. Cut yarn, tie ends, and hide tails. (Figure 1)

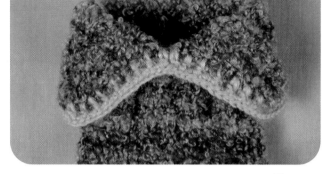

Figure 1

This project was knit with

(A) 2 balls of Schachenmayr Two in One, chunky weight, 32% wool/5% nylon/63% acrylic, 1¾oz/50g = approx 88yd/80m per ball, color #06

(B) 1 ball of Schachenmayr Mohana, chunky weight, 33% mohair/67% acrylic, 1¾oz/50g = approx 137yd/125m per ball, color #24

Totally Toe Socks

Few things are as cool on a crisp autumn day as showing off your favorite pair of socks. Wear these toe socks with chunky leather sandals to give them maximum exposure.

EXPERIENCE LEVEL

■■■▷ EXPERIENCED

SIZES

Woman's small/medium (woman's large)

LENGTH ON LEG

Below the knee

MATERIALS AND TOOLS

Yarn A (SUPER FINE **1**): 478yd/438m (717yd/657m) of Fine weight yarn, wool/polyamide, in variegated blue and gray

Yarn B (LACE **0**): 239yd/219m of Lace weight yarn, wool/polyamide, in variegated green, gray, and blue
Knitting needles: Set of 5 dpn, 3 mm (size 3 U.S.) *or size to obtain gauge*
Crochet hook: 3.5 mm (E/4)
2 holders
Scissors
Tapestry needle

GAUGE

12 sts and 17 rows = 2"/5cm with Yarn A in Stockinette Stitch
13 sts and 17 rows = 2"/5cm with Yarn B in Rib Stitch
Always take time to check your gauge.

Instructions

CUFF

With Yarn B, CO 56 (64) sts.

Divide sts evenly between 4 needles—14 (16) sts on each needle.

Work around in k2, p2 rib for 30 (40) rnds, or desired length to beg of leg.

LEG

Join Yarn A, and work in St st (k all sts) for 90 (100) rnds.

Rep dec rnd three times, in rnds 11, 31, 61 (15, 39, 67).

Dec rnd: On each needle: K to last 2 sts, skp.

Now you have 11 (13) sts on each needle—44 (52) sts total.

HEEL FLAP

Join Yarn B, and using spare needle, sl 1, k across sts from Needle 4, then Needle 1—21(25) sts; leave sts on Needles 2 and 3 unworked.

Work back and forth in St st (k1 row, p1 row) for 19 (23) rows. End with WS row.

HEEL

Work short rows as foll:
Sl 1, k13 (16), skp, turn;
*sl 1, p6 (8), p2tog, turn;
sl 1, k6 (8), skp, turn.

Rep from * until all sts have been worked—8 (10) sts on your needle.

Join Yarn A,

Next row (RS): K4 (5) sts onto Needle 4, then k4 (5) sts onto Needle 1.

GUSSET

Using Needle 1, pick up and k11 (12) sts evenly spaced along edge of heel.

Cont to work in-the-rnd, and k sts on Needles 2 and 3.

Using spare needle, pick up and k11 (12) sts evenly spaced along edge of heel, then k4 (5) sts from Needle 4—15 (17) sts on Needles 1 and 4.

INSTEP

*Rnd 1: K all sts.

Rnd 2: Needle 1: K to last 3 sts, skp, k1; Needles 2 and 3: K all sts; Needle 4: K1, k2tog, k to end.

Rep from * four times, until 11 (13) sts rem on Needles 1 and 4—44 (52) sts total.

FOOT

Work around in k for 40 (50) rnds, or desired length to beg of toe.

TOE—RIGHT SOCK

Work as follows:

Needle 1: K all sts; Needle 2: K all sts, then k another 4 (4) sts from Needle 3.

Join Yarn B, and using spare needle, k7 (9) sts rem from Needle 3, then k7 (9) sts from Needle 4, then CO 2 more sts.

There are 16 (20) sts onto spare needle.

Move onto first holder rem 4 (4) sts from Needle 4, then all sts from Needle 1.
Move onto second holder all sts from Needle 2.

There are 15 (17) sts on each holder.

Divide big toe sts (sts from spare needle) between 4 needles—4 (5) sts on each needle.

To divide the sts, move 1st 3 (4) sts from spare needle onto Needle 1, next 4 (5) sts onto Needle 2, next 4 (5) sts onto Needle 3, next 4 (5) sts onto Needle 4, and last CO st onto Needle 1 again.

Work around in St st (k all sts) for 12 (14) rnds.

Dec rnd: Needles 1 and 3: K2tog, k to end; Needles 2 and 4: K to last 2 sts, skp.

Work dec rnd until 2 sts rem on each needle.

Cut yarn, leaving a 10"/25cm tail. Thread the needle with the tail and *insert through all sts, from 1st to last. Draw yarn back through all sts and tighten. Rep from * twice. Cut yarn, tie ends, and hide tails.

Continue to "End at the toe—both socks".

TOE—LEFT SOCK
Work as follows:

Move 1st 4 (4) sts from Needle 1 onto Needle 4.

Join Yarn B, and using spare needle, k7 (9) sts rem from Needle 1, then k7 (9) sts from Needle 2, then CO 2 more sts.

There are 16 (20) sts onto spare needle.

Move onto first holder rem 4 (4) sts from Needle 2, then all sts from Needle 3. Move onto second holder all sts from Needle 4.

There are 15 (17) sts on each holder.

Divide big toe sts (sts from spare needle) between 4 needles—4 (5) sts on each needle.

To divide the sts, move 1st 3 (4) sts from spare needle onto Needle 1, next 4 (5) sts onto Needle 2, next 4 (5) sts onto Needle 3, next 4 (5) sts onto Needle 4, and last CO st onto Needle 1 again.

Work around in St st (k all sts) for 12 (14) rnds (Figure 1).

Dec rnd: Needles 1 and 3: K2tog, k to end; Needles 2 and 4: K to last 2 sts, skp.

Work dec rnd until 2 sts rem on each needle.

Cut yarn, leaving a 10"/25cm tail. Thread the needle with the tail and *insert through all sts, from 1st to last. Draw yarn back through all sts and tighten. Rep from * twice. Cut yarn, tie ends, and hide tails.

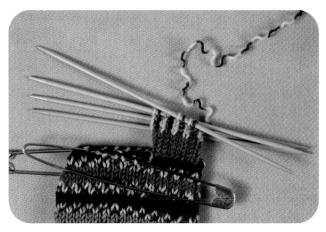

Figure 1

Figure 2

END AT THE TOE—BOTH SOCKS

Beg from the sts closest to the toe, and move 7 (8) sts from 1st holder onto Needle 1, then another 8 (9) rem sts onto Needle 2.

Move 8 (9) next sts from second holder onto Needle 3, then 7 (8) rem sts onto Needle 4.

With Yarn A, and using Needle 4, pick up and k2 more sts, inserting needle into CO sts of the toe. Move last CO sts from Needle 4 onto Needle 1. There are now 8 (9) sts on each needle.

*Rnd 1: K all sts.

Rnd 2 (dec rnd): Needles 2 and 4: K to last 3 sts, skp, k; Needles 1 and 3: K1, k2tog, k to end.

Rep from * until 2 sts rem on each needle.

Cut yarn, leaving a 10"/25cm tail. Thread the needle with the tail and *insert through all sts, from 1st to last. Draw yarn back through all sts and tighten. Rep from * twice. Cut yarn, tie ends, and hide tails. (Figure 2)

This project was knit with

(A) 2 balls (3 balls) of Schachenmayr Regia Jacquard 4 Ply, lace weight, 75% wool/25% polyamide, 1¾oz/50g = approx 239yd/219m per ball, color #5274

(B) 1 ball of Schachenmayr Regia Jacquard 4 Ply, lace weight, 75% wool/25% polyamide, 1¾oz/50g = approx 239yd/219m per ball, color #5272

Mary's Little Lamb Socks

Mary had just one little lamb, but with these adorable socks, you'll have a pair! These lambs will keep little feet snug and stylish wherever they wander!

EXPERIENCE LEVEL

■■■▬ EXPERIENCED

SIZES

Woman's extra small (woman's small, woman's medium)

LENGTH ON LEG

Lower calf

MATERIALS AND TOOLS

Yarn A [MEDIUM 4] : 306yd/280m of Medium weight yarn, cotton/extra fine merino/polyamide, in purple

Yarn B [SUPER BULKY 6] : 16yd/15m of Super bulky weight yarn, wool/acrylic/polyamide, in variegated gray and cream

Yarn C [MEDIUM 4] : 153yd/140m of Medium weight yarn, cotton/extra fine merino/polyamide, in violet

Knitting needles: Set of 5 dpn, 3 mm (size 3 U.S.) *or size to obtain gauge*

Crochet hook: 3.5 mm (E/4)

Scissors

Tapestry needle

Sewing needle and thread

4 black beads, ¼"/1cm in diameter

2 small silver bells

GAUGE

14 sts and 18 rows = 2"/5cm with Yarn A in Stockinette Stitch

14 sts and 18 rows = 2"/5cm with Yarn A in Rib Pattern

Always take time to check your gauge.

Instructions

LAMB PATTERN

RNDS

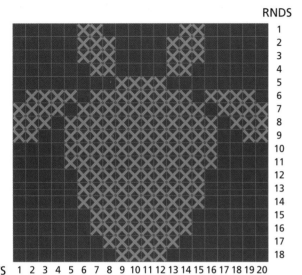

STS

Lamb Pattern Key
■ - MC is Yarn A
✕ - CC is Yarn C

NOTE: *For a tidy interior, cut Yarn C after each round and join again at the beginning of the next round. Tie tails every two rounds, and take care not to pull the yarn too tightly.*

CUFF
With Yarn A, CO 40 (44, 48) sts.

Divide sts between 4 needles—10 (11, 12) sts on each needle.

Work around in k1, p1 rib for 4 rnds.

Join Yarn B. *K all sts for 1 rnd.

With Yarn A, k all sts for 1 rnd.

Rep from * five times.

LEG
With Yarn A, k all sts for 6 rnds, then work around in k following Lamb Pattern for 18 rnds. Pattern consists of 18 rnds and 20 sts. Needles 1 and 4: K all sts; Needles 2 and 3: Work in pattern on 20 middle sts.

NOTE: *You may find it easier to transfer 20 stitches from Needles 2 and 3 to a single needle while working in pattern. Transfer remaining 0 (2, 4) stitches from Needle 2 to Needle 1, and remaining 0 (2, 4) stitches from Needle 3 to Needle 4.*

Cont with Yarn A, and k all sts for 10 rnds, or desired length to beg of heel flap. End at Needle 3.

HEEL FLAP

Join Yarn B, and using spare needle, sl 1, k across sts from Needle 4, then Needle 1—19 (21, 23) sts; leave sts on Needles 2 and 3 unworked.

Join Yarn C and work back and forth in St st (k1 row, p1 row) for 15 more rows. End with a WS row.

....

HEEL

With Yarn C, work short rows as follows:
Sl 1, k12 (13, 14), skp, turn;
*sl 1, p6 (6, 6), p2tog, turn;
sl 1, k6 (6, 6), skp, turn.

Rep from * until all sts have been worked—8 (8, 8) sts on your needle.

Next row (RS): With Yarn A, k4 (4, 4) sts onto Needle 4, then onto Needle 1.

....

GUSSET

Using Needle 1, pick up and k11 (12, 13) sts evenly spaced along edge of heel.

Cont to work in-the-rnd and k sts on Needles 2 and 3.

Using spare needle, pick up and k11 (12, 13) sts evenly spaced along edge of heel, then k4 (4, 4) sts from Needle 4—15 (16, 17) sts on Needles 1 and 4.

....

INSTEP

*Rnd 1: K all sts.

Rnd 2: Needle 1: K to last 3 sts, skp, k1; Needles 2 and 3: K all sts; Needle 4: K1, k2tog, k to end.

Rep from * five times, until 10 (11, 12) sts rem on each needle.

....

FOOT

Work around in k for 26 (32, 38) rnds.

Work 1 more rnd as follows: Needles 1 and 4: With Yarn A, k all sts; Needles 2 and 3: Join Yarn B and k all sts.

....

TOE

Join Yarn C,

Rnd 1: K all sts.

*Rnd 2 (dec rnd): Needles 1 and 3: K to last 3 sts, skp, k1; Needles 2 and 4: K1, k2tog, k to end.

Rep from * until 7 (8, 8) sts rem on each needle.

Now rep rnd 2 every rnd until 3 sts rem on each needle.

Cut yarn, leaving a 10"/25cm tail. Thread the needle with the tail and *insert through all sts, from 1st to last. Draw yarn back through all sts and tighten. Rep from * twice. Cut yarn, tie ends, and hide tails.

....

Figure 1

Figure 2

Finishing

CROCHETED EDGING

With RS facing, cuff away from you, and Yarn C, insert hook under 1st CO st and *ch 1, sl st under next CO st. Rep from * around top of sock. Cut yarn, tie ends, and hide tails. (Figure 1)

NOSE, EYES, AND BELL

Find the middle of the lamb's face and sew a few simple stitches with the black thread to make a protruding nose. Count a few rows up from the nose and sew on 2 black beads for the eyes. Draw the thread through each bead several times to secure tightly. Sew on the bell at the bottom of the lamb's chin. (Figure 2)

This project was knit with

(A) 2 balls of Gedifra Airmix, 30% cotton/62% extra fine merino/8% polyamide, Aran weight, 1¾oz/50g = approx 153yd/140m per ball, color #7046

(B) 1 ball of Gedifra Sheela, 48% wool/48% acrylic/4% polyamide, super bulky weight, 1¾oz/50g = approx 32yd/30m per ball, color #4193

(C) 1 ball of Gedifra Airmix, 30% cotton/62% extra fine merino/8% polyamide, Aran weight, 1¾oz/50g = approx 153yd/140m per ball, color #7037

Square Crocheted Knee Socks

The technique in this pattern is a little different than in other patterns since the sock is crocheted and the cuff, heel, and toe are knitted.

EXPERIENCE LEVEL

■■■□ EXPERIENCED

SIZES

Woman's small/medium

LENGTH ON LEG

Below the knee

MATERIALS AND TOOLS

Yarn A [MEDIUM 4] : 656yd/600m of Medium weight yarn, nylon/acrylic/kid mohair, in red

Yarn B [MEDIUM 4] : 164yd/150m of Medium weight yarn, nylon/acrylic/kid mohair, in black
Crochet hook: 3.5 mm (E/4) *or size to obtain gauge*
Knitting needles: Set of 5 dpn, 3 mm (size 3 U.S.) *or size to obtain gauge*
Scissors
Tapestry needle

GAUGE

5 squares and 4 rows = 2"/5cm with Yarn A in Square Net Pattern
10 sts and 12 rows = 2"/5cm with 2 strands of Yarn B in Rib Stitch
10 sts and 12 rows = 2"/5cm with 2 strands of Yarn A in Stockinette Stitch
Always take time to check your gauge.

Instructions

NOTE: *In this design, you'll crochet the leg first, then add a knitted cuff, gusset, and toe.*

LEG

Base row: With hook and Yarn A, ch 52 sts. Sl st in 1st ch to join.

Rnd 1: Ch 4, skip next ch, dc into next ch. *Ch 1, skip next ch, dc into next ch. Rep from * twenty-five times. Ch 1, sl st into 3rd ch from beg of rnd—25 dc in total.

Rnds 2–16: Ch 4, dc into next dc of prev rnd. *Ch 1, dc into next dc of prev rnd. Rep from * twenty-five times. Ch 1, sl st into 3rd ch from beg of rnd—25 dc in total.

HEEL FLAP

With RS facing, top close to you, using 2 strands of Yarn B and knitting needles, pick up and k24 sts, inserting needle into 12 dc sts and 12 ch sts between them.

Work in St st (k1 row, p1 row) for 15 more rows. End with a WS row.

HEEL

Work short rows as follows:
Sl 1, k14, skp, turn;
*sl 1, p6, p2tog, turn;
sl 1, k6, skp, turn.

Rep from * until all sts have been worked—8 sts on your needle (Figure 1). BO all sts.

GUSSET

With RS facing, bottom of sock away from you and back of the leg upwards, join Yarn A.

Rnd 1: Insert hook into right corner of gusset. Ch 4, dc in 3rd st from hook along edge of gusset. *Ch 1, dc in 3rd st from hook.

Rep from * six times along right edge of gusset. (Figure 2)

Turn sock over and rep seven more times along left edge of gusset until you reach the left corner.

Cont to work-in-the-rnd as follows:

*Ch 1, dc in next dc of prev round.

Rep from * fourteen times.

Ch 1, sl st into 3rd ch from beg of rnd.

Rnd 2 (dec rnd): Ch 4, dc in next dc of prev rnd.

*Ch 1, dc in next dc of prev rnd. Rep from * twelve times.

*Dc 1 in next dc. Rep from * two times.

*Ch 1, dc 1 in next dc of prev rnd. Rep from * twelve times.

Dc 1 in next dc. Sl st into 3rd ch from beg of rnd.

Rnd 3 (dec rnd): Ch 4, dc 1 in next dc of prev rnd.

*Ch 1, dc 1 in next dc of prev rnd. Rep from * twelve times.

Ch 1, dc 1 in 2nd dc from hook.

*Ch 1, dc 1 in next dc of prev rnd. Rep from * twelve times.

Ch 1, sl st into 3rd ch from beg of rnd.

FOOT

Work around as follows for 6 rounds, or desired length to beg of toe:

Rnds 1–6: Ch 4, dc into next dc of prev rnd. *Ch 1, dc into next dc of prev rnd.

Rep from * twenty-five times.

Ch 1, sl st into 3rd ch from beg of rnd.

TOE

With RS facing, sole up, toe away from you, using 2 strands of Yarn B and dpn, beg at middle of sole and pick up and k52 sts. Divide sts evenly between four needles—13 sts on each needle.

NOTE: *Insert needle into every ch and dc st.*

*Rnd 1: K all sts.

Rnd 2 (dec rnd): Needles 1 and 3: K to last 3 sts, skp, k1; Needles 2 and 4: K1, k2tog, k to end.

Rep from * until 10 sts rem on each needle.

Rep rnd 2 every rnd until 3 sts rem on each needle.

Cut yarn, leaving a 10"/25cm tail. Thread the needle with the tail and *insert through all sts, from 1st to last. Draw yarn back through all sts and tighten. Rep from * twice. Cut yarn, tie ends, and hide tails.

CUFF

With RS facing, gusset up, top away from you, using 2 strands of Yarn B and dpn, beg at middle of back of leg and pick up and k52 sts. Divide sts evenly between four needles—13 sts on each needle.

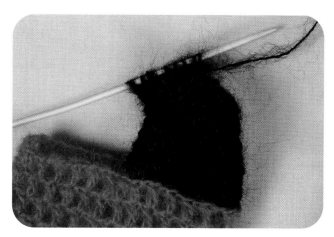

Figure 1

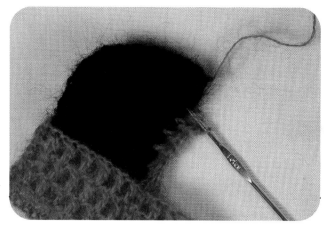

Figure 2

NOTE: *Insert needle into every ch and dc st.*

Work around in k1, p1 rib for 20 rnds or any desired length. BO in Rib st.

This project was knit with

(A) 2 balls of Schachenmayr Kid Light, Aran weight, 35% nylon/35% acrylic/30% kid mohair, 1¾oz/50g = approx 328yd/300m per ball, color #30
(B) 1 ball of Schachenmayr Kid Light, Aran weight, 35% nylon/35% acrylic/30% kid mohair, 1¾oz/50g = approx 328yd/300m per ball, color #99

Fluffy Slippers

Curl up with a good book—and a great pair of slippers.
These are fluffy on top and sturdy on the bottom.

EXPERIENCE LEVEL

■■■☐ INTERMEDIATE

SIZES

Woman's small (woman's medium, woman's large)

LENGTH ON LEG

Above the ankle

MATERIALS AND TOOLS

Yarn A **[BULKY 5]**: 137yd/125m of Bulky weight yarn, mohair/acrylic, in apricot and gray blend

Yarn B **[BULKY 5]**: 77yd//70m of Bulky weight yarn, polyamide, in apricot
Knitting needles: Set of 5 dpn, 4 mm (size 6 U.S.) *or size to obtain gauge*
Crochet hook: 3.5 mm (E/4)
Tracing paper, pencil, and permanent marker
Scissors
Black leather square, 12 x 12"/30 x 30cm
Leather hole punch, 3mm hole
Sewing needle and thread
Tapestry needle

GAUGE

10 sts and 13 rows = 2"/5cm with Yarn A in Stockinette Stitch
9 sts and 13 rows = 2"/5cm with Yarn A in Rib Stitch
Always take time to check your gauge.

Instructions

Figure 1

Figure 2

Figure 3

CUFF

With Yarn A, CO 40 (48, 56) sts.

Divide sts evenly between 4 needles —10 (12, 14) sts on each needle.

Work around in k2, p2 rib for 18 (20, 26) rnds.

LEG

Join Yarn B and work around in St st (k all sts) for 10 (10, 14) rnds, or desired length.

UPPER

Using spare needle, k all sts from Needle 1, and 1 (2, 2) sts from Needle 2.

Join Yarn A, and using spare needle, k18 (20, 24) sts as follows: 9 (10, 12) from Needle 2 and 9 (10, 12) from Needle 3.

Transfer rem 1 (2, 2) sts from Needle 3 onto Needle 4; leave sts on Needles 1 and 4 unworked.

Work in St st back and forth (k1 row, p1 row) for 31 (39, 47) rows (Figure 1). End with WS row.

BASE

With Yarn B and using spare needle, pick up and k16 (20, 24) sts evenly spaced along right edge of top of the foot (Figure 2). Using same needle, k 1st 9 (10, 12) sts from Needle 2. Using spare needle, k rem 9 (10, 12) sts, then pick up and k16 (20, 24) sts evenly spaced along left edge along top of foot.

Using spare needle, k all sts from Needle 4.

There are now 72 (88, 104) sts in total: 11 (14, 16) sts on Needles 1 and 4, and 25 (30, 36) sts on Needles 2 and 3 total.

Divide sts evenly between 4 needles as follows:

Place 1st 7 (8, 10) sts from Needle 2 on Needle 1.
Place last 7 (8, 10) sts from Needle 3 on Needle 4.
There are now 18 (22, 26) sts on each needle.

Work-in-the-rnd and k all sts for 12 (14, 16) rnds. BO all sts.

Finishing

Sole

With the pencil, copy the appropriate sole template (pages 126-127) onto tracing paper. Mark 3 mm holes all around the template edge, ¼"/0.6cm from the edge and ¼"/0.6cm apart from each other. When spacing the holes, measure the space between each hole from the middle of the holes. Cut out, transfer to leather square, trace around template with the permanent marker, and cut out leather sole. Punch 3mm holes as marked.

Position the sole on the bottom of the slipper. Orient the leather with the smooth side upwards, so that you don't slip while walking. With the needle and thread, secure the sole in place by making loose stitches all around. (Figure 3)

With sole away from you, heel up, and Yarn A,

Rnd 1: Insert hook under 1st BO st of slipper, and through the closest hole in the sole. Ch 1, then sc 1 under BO sts and through holes in the sole all around the foot to connect the sole to the slipper. End with sl st through 1st sc.

Rnd 2: Ch 1, sc 1 through each sc around the sole. When you reach a corner, sc 2 through every sc, then cont with sc 1 through each sc until the next corner. End with sl st through 1st sc.

To finish, cut a ½ x 1½"/1 x 4cm piece of leather (use leftover leather from cutting the sole). With leather punch, make 2 holes on both short ends of the leather. Fold the leather over the top of the slipper at the center back, and sew in place using Yarn A.

This project was knit with

(A) 1 ball of Schachenmayr Mohana Color, chunky weight, 33% mohair/67% acrylic, 1¾oz/50g = approx 137yd/125m per ball, color #89
(B) 2 balls of Schachenmayr Cassiopeia, chunky weight, 100% polyamide, 1¾oz/50g = approx 77yd/70m per ball, color #26

Mutt-ering Around Slippers

Take these puppies for a walk around your house. Friendly and fuzzy, they're perfect for puttering around in all day long!

EXPERIENCE LEVEL

■■■□ INTERMEDIATE

SIZES

Woman's small (woman's medium, woman's large)

LENGTH ON LEG

Above the ankle

MATERIALS AND TOOLS

BULKY

Yarn A **5** : 115 (154, 192)yd/105 (140, 175)m of Bulky weight yarn, polyamide, in black and white

SUPER BULKY

Yarn B **6** : 55yd/50m of Super bulky weight yarn, merino wool/acrylic/polyamide, in cream

SUPER BULKY

Yarn C **6** : 11yd/10m of Super bulky weight yarn, merino wool/acrylic/polyamide, in black

Knitting needles: Set of 5 dpn, 4 mm (size 6 U.S.) *or size to obtain gauge*

Crochet hook: 3.5 mm (E/4)

Scissors

Tapestry needle

Stitch marker

4 round red buttons, ½"/1.3cm in diameter

4 round black buttons, ¼"/0.6cm in diameter

Sewing needle and thread

GAUGE

17 sts and 26 rows = 4"/10cm with Yarn A in Stockinette Stitch

17 sts and 24 rows = 4"/10cm with Yarn B in Rib Stitch

Always take time to check your gauge.

Instructions

CUFF
With Yarn B, CO 36 (40, 44) sts.

Divide sts evenly between 4 needles—9 (10, 11) sts on each needle.

Work around in k1, p1 rib for 5 rnds, or desired length to beg of leg.

LEG
K all sts for 1 rnd. Cut Yarn B.

Join Yarn A and work in St st (k all sts) for 12 rnds, or desired length to beg of heel flap. End at Needle 3.

HEEL FLAP
Using spare needle, sl 1, k across sts from Needle 4, then Needle 1—17 (19, 21) sts; leave sts on Needles 2 and 3 unworked.

Work back and forth in St st (k1 row, p1 row) for 11 (13, 15) more rows. End with WS row.

HEEL
Work short rows as follows:
Sl 1, k10 (12, 13), skp, turn;
*sl 1, p4 (6, 6), p2tog, turn;
sl 1, k4 (6, 6) skp, turn.

Rep from * until all sts have been worked—6 (8, 8) sts on your needle.

Next row (RS): K3 (4, 4) sts onto Needle 4, then k3 (4, 4) sts onto Needle 1.

GUSSET
Using Needle 1, pick up and k9 (9, 10) sts evenly spaced along edge of heel.

Cont to work in-the-rnd, and k sts on Needles 2 and 3.

Using spare needle, pick up and k9 (9, 10) sts evenly spaced along edge of heel, then k3 (4, 4) sts from Needle 4—12 (13, 14) sts on Needles 1 and 4.

INSTEP
*Rnd 1: Needle 1: K to last 3 sts, skp, k1; Needles 2 and 3: K all sts; Needle 4: K1, k2tog, k to end.

Rnd 2: K all sts.

Rep from * three times, until there are 9 (10, 11) sts on Needles 1 and 4—36 (40, 44) sts total.

FOOT
Work around in k for 30 (34, 36) rnds, or desired length to beg of toe.

TOE
*Rnd 1: K all sts.

Rnd 2 (dec rnd): Needles 1 and 3: K to last 3 sts, skp, k1; Needles 2 and 4: K1, k2tog, k to end.

Rep from * until 7 (7, 8) sts rem on each needle.

Now rep rnd 2 every rnd until 6 sts rem on each needle. Cut Yarn A.

Join Yarn B and rep rnd 2 until 4 sts rem on each needle. Cut Yarn B.

Join Yarn C and rep rnd 2 until 3 sts rem on each needle.

Cut yarn, leaving a 10"/25cm tail. Thread the needle with the tail and *insert through all sts, from 1st to last. Draw yarn back through all sts and tighten. Rep from * twice. Cut yarn, tie ends, and hide tails.

Finishing

With RS facing and toe away from you, mark top center of sock.

Right ear
Row 1: Count one row from the cuff and six ribs to the right of center. Hold Yarn B inside and insert hook from front to back. Ch 1 then sc 1 through each of following 3 sts towards center.

Row 2: Ch 1, then sc 2 in 1st sc, sc 1 in 2nd sc, sc 2 in 3rd sc.

Rows 3–10: Ch 1, sc 1 in each sc of prev row (5 sc total).

Row 11 (dec row): Ch 1, sc 1 in 2nd sc of prev row, sc 1 into next st, sc 1 in last st. Turn and sl st all along top edge. Cut yarn, tie ends, and hide tails.

Left ear
Row 1: Count third k st to the left of center and insert hook. With Yarn B, ch 1, then sc 1 through each of following 3 sts away from center. (Figure 1)

Follow same instructions for right ear, rows 2–11, to make left ear.

Crocheted ear edging
With toe away from you and Yarn A, insert hook in bottom right corner of right ear, and through sock. Ch 1, then sc 1 (through ear only) in each st along edge of ear. (Figure 2) Cont until bottom left corner of ear. Sl st through ear and sock. Cut yarn, tie ends, and hide tails.

Figure 1

Figure 2

Figure 3

Follow same instructions to make edging on left ear.

Eyes
Measure 1½"/4cm under cuff at front center of sock. Sew a red bead just to the right of center. Sew the other red bead to the left of the 1st bead. Sew on the black beads in front of the red beads. (Figure 3)

This project was knit with

(A) 2 (2, 3) balls of Schachenmayr Cassiopeia, chunky weight, 100% polyamide yarn, 1¾oz/50g = approx 77yd/70m, color #90
(B) 1 ball of Gedifra Boheme, bulky weight, 43% merino wool/43% acrylic/14% polyamide yarn, 1¾oz/50g = approx 109yd/100m, color #1825
(C) 1 ball of Gedifra Boheme, bulky weight, 43% merino wool/43% acrylic/14% polyamide, 1¾oz/50g = approx 109yd/100m per ball, color #1814

Autumn Slippers

Warm and rugged, this slipper is perfect for padding around the cottage on a chilly autumn morning.

EXPERIENCE LEVEL

■■■□ EXPERIENCED

SIZES

Woman's small (woman's medium, woman's large)

LENGTH ON LEG

Below the ankle

MATERIALS AND TOOLS

Yarn A **SUPER BULKY 6**: 120yd/110m of Bulky weight yarn, wool/acrylic, in variegated blue, green, and brown

Yarn B **MEDIUM 4**: 38yd/35m of Super bulky weight yarn, wool/acrylic/polyamide, in beige

Yarn C **MEDIUM 4**: 27yd/25m of Medium weight yarn, wool/acrylic/polyamide, in green

Yarn D **MEDIUM 4**: 27yd/25m of Medium weight yarn, wool/acrylic/polyamide, in teal

Crochet hook: 3.5 mm (E/4) *or size to obtain gauge*

Tracing paper, pencil, and permanent marker

Scissors

Brown leather square, 12 x 12"/30 x 30cm

Leather hole punch, 3mm hole

Tapestry needle

GAUGE

8 sts and 6 rows = 2"/5cm with Yarn A or B in Single Crochet

Always take time to check your gauge.

Instructions

Figure 1

Figure 2

SOLE

With the pencil, copy the appropriate sole template (pages 126-127) onto tracing paper. Mark 3 mm holes all around the template edge, ¼"/0.6cm from the edge and ¼"/0.6cm apart from each other. When spacing the holes, measure the space between each hole from the middle of the holes. Cut out, transfer to leather square, trace around template with the permanent marker, and cut out leather sole. Punch 3mm holes as marked.

Orient the leather with the smooth side upwards (so that you don't slip while walking). Position the heel away from you.

Rnd 1: With Yarn A, insert hook in top hole at middle back of sole (the heel) and ch 1. Sc 1 in every hole around the sole. (Figure 1) Sc 2 in the hole at each curve to prevent sole from crumpling. End with sl st through 1st sc.

AROUND THE FOOT

Rnds 2–6: Ch 1, sc in the front loop of each sc of prev rnd all around the base (Figure 2). Sl st in front loop of 1st sc from beg of rnd. Don't cut yarn, as you will use it to finish the upper.

UPPER

With toe close to you and sole down, find middle front of slipper and count 4 (5, 6) sts on either side of center st for a total of 9 (11, 13) middle sts total.

With Yarn B, insert hook in back loop of the rightmost middle st.

Row 1: Ch 1, then sc 8 (10, 12) in back loop of rem 8 (10, 12) middle sts. Rotate slipper so toe is away from you.

Rows 2, 4, 6, 8, 10, 12, 14 (16), (16, 18, 20): Insert hook in front loop of 2nd sc from hook in top rnd of base (Figure 3). Pull yarn through this st and st on the hook. Ch 1, sc 1 in each st of prev row across top of slipper—10 (12, 14) sc in total. Rotate slipper so toe is close to you.

Rows 3, 5, 7, 9, 11, 13 (15), (15, 17, 19): Insert hook in back loop of 2nd sc from hook in top rnd of base. Pull yarn through this st and st on the hook. Ch 1, sc 1 in each st of prev row across top of slipper—10 (12, 14) sc in total. Rotate slipper so toe is away from you.

Insert hook in back loop of 2nd sc from hook in top round of the base. Pull yarn through this st and st on the hook. Cut yarn, tie ends, and hide tails.

Figure 3

LEG
Rnd 1: With Yarn A and starting at the middle back of the slipper, ch 1, sc in back loop of each sc at top of base until you reach the right corner of the upper.

Sc in each sc of the upper until you reach the left corner of the upper (Figure 4). Cont sc in back loop of each sc until end of rnd. End with sl st in back loop of 1st sc from beg of rnd.

Rnd 2: Ch 1, sc in back loop of each sc of prev rnd all around leg opening. End with sl st in back loop of 1st sc from beg of rnd.

Figure 4

To make the socks higher on the leg, rep rnd 2 desired number of times.

Rnd 3: With Yarn B, ch 1, sc in back loop of each sc of prev rnd all around leg opening. End with sl st in back loop of 1st sc from beg of rnd.

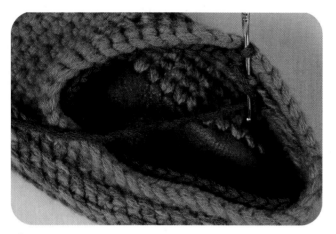

Figure 5

Figure 6

Figure 7

FAUX SOCK

With toe away from you, sole down, and Yarn C (or Yarn D), Rnd 1: Starting at middle back of the slipper, insert hook in back loop of st 1 row before top rnd of leg opening. Pull yarn through, ch 1, sc all around leg opening. (Figure 5) End with sl st in 1st sc from beg of rnd.

Rnds 2–3: Ch 1, sc 1 in each sc of prev rnd. End with sl st in 1st sc.

UPPER EDGING

With toe to the right, sole down, and Yarn B, begin at the bottom corner closest to the leg opening and insert hook upwards in front loop of last base row. Ch 1, sc in each front loop of sc in last base row all along the upper. (Figure 6) Sl st along upper edge. Cut yarn, tie ends, and hide tails.

SOLE EDGING

With sole down, heel away from you and Yarn B, insert hook downwards in front loop of sc in 1st rnd of base. Ch 1, sc 1 in each front loop of sc of 1st rnd of base all around sole. (Figure 7) End with sl st in 1st sc. Cut yarn, tie ends, and hide tails.

This project was knit with

(A) 2 balls of Schachenmayr Boston Multi Color, bulky weight, 30% wool/70% acrylic, 1¾oz/50g = approx 60yd/55m per ball, color #188

(B) 1 ball of Schachenmayr Boston, bulky weight, 30% wool/70% acrylic, 1¾oz/50g = approx 60yd/55m per ball, color #11

(C) 1 ball of Gedifra Shanina, worsted weight, 30% wool/30% acrylic/40% polyamide, 1¾oz/50g = approx 82yd /75m per ball, color #5078

Laced Legwarmers

These colorful leg warmers add a fashionable touch to a simple skirt. Wrap the leather lace around the thigh a couple of times, then tie with a bow at the front to complete the effect.

EXPERIENCE LEVEL

■□□□ BEGINNER

SIZES

Woman's small (woman's medium, woman's large)

LENGTH ON LEG

Below the knee

MATERIALS AND TOOLS

Yarn A **BULKY 5**: 205 (274, 342)yd/187 (250, 312)m of Bulky weight yarn, mohair/acrylic, in burgundy

Yarn B **LIGHT 3**: 66yd/60m of Light weight yarn, polyamide, in black

Yarn C **BULKY 5**: 137yd/125m of Bulky weight yarn, mohair/acrylic, in black

Yarn D **BULKY 5**: 137yd/125m of Bulky weight yarn, mohair/acrylic, in rose

Yarn E **BULKY 5**: 137yd/125m of Bulky weight yarn, mohair/acrylic, in variegated rose, pink, and grey

Knitting needles: Set of 5 dpn, 4 mm (size 6 U.S.) *or size to obtain gauge*

Crochet hook: 3.5 mm (E/4)

Scissors

Tapestry needle

2 black leather pieces, ½ X 1½"/1 X 4cm

Leather hole punch, 3mm hole

2 black leather laces, 60"/150cm long

GAUGE

11 sts and 14 rows = 2"/5cm with Yarn A, C, D, or E in Stockinette Stitch

Always take time to check your gauge.

Instructions

THIGH

With Yarn A, CO 60 (64, 68) sts. Divide sts evenly between 4 needles—15 (16, 17) sts on each needle.

Rnds 1-12 (1-14, 1-16): Work around in St st (k all sts).

Rnd 13 (15, 17): Join Yarn B and k all sts.

Rnd 14 (16, 18): With Yarn A, k all sts.

Rnd 15 (17, 19) (dec rnd): With Yarn B, work as follows: Needles 1, 2, 3, 4: K to last 2 sts, skp. There are now 14 (15, 16) sts on each needle.

Rnd 16 (18, 20): With Yarn A, k all sts.

Rnd 17 (19, 21): With Yarn B, k all sts.

Rnd 18 (20, 22): With Yarn A, k all sts. Cut Yarns A and B.
.

Rnds 19–21 (21–23, 23–25): Join Yarn C and p all sts.

Rnds 22–23 (24–25, 26–27): Join Yarn D and k all sts.

Rnds 24–26 (26–28, 28–30): With Yarn C, p all sts.

Rnds 27–28 (29–30, 31–32): With Yarn D, k all sts.

Rnds 29–31 (31–33, 33–35): With Yarn C, p all sts. Cut Yarns C and D.

Rnds 32–43 (34–47, 36–49): Join Yarn E and k all sts. Cut Yarn E.

Rnds 44–46 (48–50, 50–52): Join Yarn D and p all sts. Cut Yarn D.

Rnd 47 (51, 53): Join Yarn C and k all sts.

Rnd 48 (52, 54) (dec rnd): With Yarn C, work as follows: Needles 1, 2, 3, 4: K to last 2 sts, skp—13 (14, 15) sts on each needle.

Rnds 49–51 (53–55, 55–57): With Yarn D, p all sts.

Rnds 52–53 (56–57, 58–59): With Yarn C, k all sts.

Rnds 54–56 (58–60, 60–62): With Yarn D, p all sts. Cut Yarns C and D.

Rnds 57–61 (61–65, 63–67): Join Yarn A and k all sts. Cut Yarn A.

Rnds 62–64 (66–68, 68–70): Join Yarn B and p all sts. Cut Yarn B.

Rnds 65–69 (69–73, 71–75): Join Yarn A and k all sts. Cut Yarn A.

Rnds 70–72 (74–76, 76–78): Join Yarn D and p all sts.

Rnds 73–74 (77–78, 79–80): Join Yarn C and k all sts.

Rnds 75–77 (79–81, 81–83): With Yarn D, p all sts.

Rnds 78–79 (82–83, 84–85): With Yarn C, p all sts.

Rnds 80–82 (84–86, 86–88): With Yarn D, p all sts. Cut Yarns C and D.

Rnds 83–96 (87-102, 89-104): Join Yarn E and k all sts.

Rnd 97 (103, 105) (dec rnd): With Yarn E, work as follows: Needles 1, 2, 3, 4: K to last 2 sts, skp. There are now 12 (13, 14) sts on each needle. Cut Yarn E.

Rnds 98–100 (104–106, 106–108): Join Yarn C and p all sts.

Rnds 101–102 (107–108, 109–110): With Yarn D, k all sts.

Rnds 103–105 (109–111, 111–113): With Yarn C, p all sts.

Rnds 106–107 (112–113, 114–115): With Yarn D, k all sts.

Rnds 108–110 (114–116, 116–118): With Yarn C, p all sts. Cut Yarns C and D.

Rnd 111 (117, 119): Join Yarn A and k all sts.

Rnd 112 (118, 120): Join Yarn B and k all sts.

Rnd 113 (119,121): With Yarn A, k all sts.

Rnd 114 (120, 122): With Yarn B, k all sts.

Rnd 115 (121, 123): With Yarn A, k all sts.

Rnd 116 (122, 124): With Yarn B, k all sts. Cut Yarn B.

Rnds 117-131 (123–139, 125–143): With Yarn A, k all sts.

BO all sts. Cut yarn, tie ends, and hide tails.

Finishing

CROCHETED EDGING
Top
With RS facing, top of leg away from you and Yarn C, insert hook under 1st CO st and ch 4, then hdc 1 into 3rd CO st from hook, ch 1, hdc 1 into 1st skipped st.

*Hdc 1 under next st, then hdc 1 into 3rd st from hook, ch 1, hdc 1 into 1st skipped st.

Rep from * all around.

End with sl st in 4th ch from beg. Cut yarn. (Figure 1)

Figure 1

Bottom

With RS facing, top of leg close to you and Yarn C, insert hook under 1st BO st and ch 4, then hdc 1 into 3rd BO from hook, ch 1, hdc 1 into 1st skipped st.

*Hdc 1 under next st, then hdc 1 into 3rd st from hook, ch 1, hdc 1 into 1st skipped st.

Rep from * all around.

End with sl st in 4th ch from beg of rnd. Cut yarn, tie ends, and hide tails.

Leather trim

With leather hole punch, make 2 holes on the shorter sides of a leather piece. Fold the leather in half over top of legwarmer at back center, and sew into place with Yarn A. Thread a leather lace through the loop. (Figure 1)

This project was knit with

(A) 2 (2, 3) balls of Schachenmayr Mohana, chunky weight, 33% mohair/67% acrylic, 1¾oz/50g = approx 137yd/125m per ball, color #32

(B) 1 ball of Schachenmayr Venuto, light weight, 100% polyamide, ¾oz/21g = approx 66yd/60m per ball, color #99

(C) 1 ball of Schachenmayr Mohana, chunky weight, 33% mohair/67% acrylic, 1¾oz/50g = approx 137yd/125m per ball, color #99

(D) 1 ball of Schachenmayr Mohana, chunky weight, 33% mohair/67% acrylic, 1¾oz/50g = approx 137yd/125m per ball, color #36

(E) 1 ball of Schachenmayr Mohana Color, chunky weight, 33% mohair/67% acrylic, 1¾oz/50g = approx 137yd/125m per ball, color #89

Sally's Seashell Crocheted Socks

This crocheted sock features a delicate shell pattern and dainty ribbon Rosebud Ribbon (page 124). Make the toe and heel in contrasting colors for a funkier look.

EXPERIENCE LEVEL

■■■▶ EXPERIENCED

SIZES

Woman's small/medium

LENGTH ON LEG

Lower calf

MATERIALS AND TOOLS

Yarn A 4 : 656yd/600m of Medium weight yarn, nylon/acrylic/kid mohair, in dark or light blue

Yarn B 4 : 164yd/150m of Medium weight yarn, nylon/acrylic/kid mohair, in apricot

Yarn C 4 : 41yd/38m of Medium weight yarn, nylon/acrylic/kid mohair, in coral
Crochet hook: 3.5 mm (E/4) *or size to obtain gauge*
Knitting needles: Set of 5 dpn, 3 mm (size 3 U.S.) *or size to obtain gauge*
Scissors
Tapestry needle

GAUGE

4 shells and 5 rows = 4"/10cm with Yarn A in Seashell Pattern
10 sts and 12 rows = 2"/5cm with 2 strands of Yarn A or B in Stockinette Stitch
Always take time to check your gauge.

Instructions

NOTE: *This sock is crocheted from the foot to the gusset, then up the leg. The toe and gusset are added afterwards.*

FOOT

Base row: With hook and Yarn A, ch 40 sts. Sl st in 1st ch to join.

Rnd 1: Ch 1, sc in each of 40 chs, sl st into 1st sc.

Rnd 2: Ch 3, (tr 1, ch 1, tr 2) all in the same sc.

*(Tr 2, ch 1, tr 2) in every 4th sc from hook.

Rep from * nine times.

Sl st in 3rd ch from beg of rnd.

Rnds 3–8: Sl st in next tr, sl st under ch.

Ch 3, (tr, ch 1, tr 2) all under same ch.

*(Tr 2, ch 1, tr 2) under each ch of prev rnd. (Figure 1)

Rep from * nine times, or desired length to heel opening.

Sl st in 3rd ch from beg of rnd.

HEEL OPENING

Start heel opening in the middle of the 1st shell as follows:

Sl st in next tr, sl st under ch of 1st shell, ch 19, sc 1 under ch of 5th shell of prev round. (Figure 2)

LEG

Cont to work-in-the-rnd as follows:

Rnd 1: Ch 3, (tr 1, ch 1, tr 2) all under same ch.

*(Tr 2, ch 1, tr 2) under each ch of prev rnd.

Rep from * seven times until 1st shell of prev rnd.

Now crochet three shells along the 19 ch that form the back of the heel opening starting with the 5th ch as follows:

*(Tr 2, ch 1, tr 2) in every 5th ch of heel opening.

Rep from * three times.

Sl st in 3rd ch from beg of rnd.

Rnds 2–6: Sl st in next tr, sl st under ch st, ch 3, (tr 1, ch 1, tr 2) all under same ch.

*(Tr 2, ch 1, tr 2) under each ch of prev rnd.

Rep from * nine times.

Sl st in 3rd ch from beg of rnd.

Make more or less rnds for desired length to toe opening of sock.

TOE OPENING

With gusset up, toe away from you and Yarn B, insert hook in middle of 1st rnd of the foot and ch 1, sc 40, all around toe opening. End with sl st in 1st sc from beg of rnd.

TOE

NOTE: *If you want your toe and gusset to blend in with the sock, use Yarn A for these parts. If you want to add a splash of color, use Yarn C.*

With RS facing, sole up, toe away from you, using 2 strands of Yarn C (Yarn A), and dpn, beg at middle of sole and pick up and k40 sts. Divide sts evenly between four needles—10 sts on each needle. (Figure 3)

NOTE: *Insert needle into each sc st.*

*Rnd 1: K all sts.

Rnd 2 (dec rnd): Needles 1 and 3: K to last 3 sts, skp, k1; Needles 2 and 4: K1, k2tog, k to end.

Rep from * until 5 sts rem on each needle.

Rep rnd 2 every rnd until 2 sts rem on each needle.

Cut yarn, leaving a 10"/25cm tail. Thread the needle with the tail and *insert through all sts, from 1st to last. Draw yarn back through all sts and tighten. Rep from * twice. Cut yarn, tie ends, and hide tails.

Figure 1

CROCHET EDGING AROUND HEEL OPENING

With RS facing, gusset to the left, heel away from you and Yarn B (Yarn A), insert hook in right corner of heel opening and ch 1, sc 20. Insert hook in each tr and under each ch of the top of the shells at the gusset.

Cont to work-in-the-rnd and sc 20, inserting hook in each ch of heel opening. Sl st in 1st sc from beg of rnd.

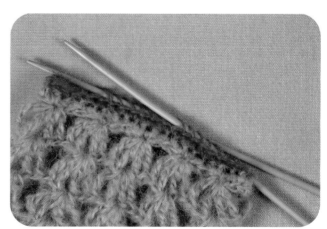

Figure 2

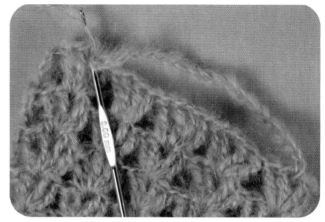

Figure 3

HEEL FLAP

With RS facing, heel opening upwards, toe away from you, using 2 strands of Yarn C (Yarn A) and dpn, pick up and k20 sts, inserting needle into each sc along the top of the gusset.

Work back and forth in St st (k1 row, p1 row) for 14 rows. End with WS row.

. . . .

HEEL

Work short rows as follows:

Sl 1, k12, skp, turn;

*sl 1, p6, p2tog, turn;

sl 1, k6, skp, turn.

Rep from * until all sts have been worked—8 sts on your needle. BO all sts.

. . . .

CONNECTING GUSSET AND FOOT

With gusset to the left, toe close to you and Yarn B, insert hook into 1st sc of edge of opening along the foot, and top right corner of gusset. Ch 1 then sc all around the gusset by inserting hook in every sc along edge of foot and every 2nd st from hook along gusset edge. (Figure 4)

At left top corner of gusset, sl st along edge of gusset. Cut yarn.

. . . .

Finishing

Leg edging

With RS facing gusset up, top away from you and Yarn C, insert hook in st of last rnd at the top and *ch 3, sl st in 1st ch, sc 1 in next st. Rep from * all around cuff. End with sl st in 1st ch from beg of rnd. Cut yarn, tie ends, and hide tails.

NOTE: *To make this edging, you'll be inserting your hook into every tr and every ch between the tr.*

. . . .

This project was knit with

(A) 2 balls of Schachenmayr Kid Light, Aran weight, 35% nylon/35% acrylic/30% kid mohair, 1¾oz/50g = approx 328yd/300m per ball, color #65 or #69

(B) 1 ball of Schachenmayr Kid Light, Aran weight, 35% nylon/35% acrylic/30% kid mohair, 1¾oz/50g = approx 328yd/300m per ball, color #27

(C) 1 ball of Schachenmayr Kid Light, Aran weight, 35% nylon/35% acrylic/30% kid mohair, 1¾oz/50g = approx 328yd/300m per ball, color #34

GUSSET

Using spare needle, pick up and k9 (11) sts evenly spaced along edge of heel.

Cont to work in-the-rnd, and work in Tree Pattern on Needles 2 and 3.

NOTE: *For shorter socks, start pattern from the 1st round. For longer socks, continue to work in pattern from the 9th round.*

Using spare needle, pick up and k9 (11) sts evenly spaced along edge of heel, then p4 (4) sts from Needle 4—13 (15) sts on Needles 1 and 4.

INSTEP

*Rnd 1: Needles 1 and 4: P all sts; Needles 2 and 3: Follow Tree Pattern.

Rnd 2: Needle 1: P to last 3 sts, p2tog, p1; Needles 2 and 3: Follow Tree Pattern; Needle 4: p1, p2tog, p to end.

Rep from * three times, until 10 (12) sts rem on each needle—40 (48) sts total.

FOOT

Work around as follows for 11 rnds for shorter socks and 3 rnds for longer socks: Needles 1 and 4: P all sts; Needles 2 and 3: Work in Tree Pattern.

NOTE: *For shorter socks, continue pattern from 8th rnd. For longer socks, continue pattern from 16th rnd. Rep pattern twice from knitting the leg until this point.*

Rnds 12–16 for shorter socks and rnds 4–8 for longer socks: Needles 1 and 4: P all sts; Needles 2 and 3: Work in Treetop Pattern for 5 rnds. Pattern consists of 14 sts and 5 rnds.

P all sts on 4 needles for 14 (22) rnds for shorter socks, or 22 (30) rnds for longer socks, or desired length to beg of toe.

TOE

Join Yarn B (Yarn A),

*Rnd 1: K all sts.

Rnd 2 (dec rnd): Needles 1 and 3: K to last 3 sts, skp, k1; Needles 2 and 4: K1, k2tog, k to end.

Rep from * until 7 (8) sts rem on each needle.

Now rep rnd 2 every rnd until 3 sts rem on each needle.

Cut yarn, leaving a 10"/25cm tail. Thread the needle with the tail and *insert through all sts, from 1st to last. Draw yarn back through all sts and tighten. Rep from * twice. Cut yarn, tie ends, and hide tails.

Finishing

Crocheted cuff edging

With RS facing you, top of cuff away from you, and Yarn B (Yarn A), insert hook under 1st CO st and ch 3, sl st into 1st ch. *Sc 1 under 2nd st from hook, ch 3, sl st into 1st ch. Rep from * all around top of sock. Sl st under 1st CO st. Cut yarn, tie ends, and hide tails.

This project was knit with

(A) 2 balls (1 ball) of Schachenmayr Mohana, 33% mohair/67% acrylic, chunky weight, 1¾oz/50g = approx 137yd/125m per ball, color #22

(B) 1 ball (2 balls) of Schachenmayr Mohana, 33% mohair/67% acrylic, chunky weight, 1¾oz/50g = approx 137yd/125m per ball, color #70

Fluffy Legwarmers

These legwarmers are knitted flat then sewn up along the seam. Fluffy and flashy, they give style to the simplest outfit.

EXPERIENCE LEVEL

■■□□ EASY

SIZES

Woman's small (woman's medium, woman's large)

LENGTH ON LEG

Below the knee

MATERIALS AND TOOLS

Yarn A **MEDIUM 4**: 88yd/80m of Medium weight yarn, polyamide, in variegated pink and brown

Yarn B **BULKY 5**: 66yd/60m of Bulky weight yarn, acrylic/wool, in variegated pastel

Yarn C **BULKY 5**: 137yd/125m of Bulky weight yarn, mohair/acrylic, in burgundy

Knitting needles:

Pair of 5 mm (size 8 U.S.) straight needles *or size to obtain gauge*

Pair of 4 mm (size 6 U.S.) straight needles *or size to obtain gauge*

Crochet hook: 3.5 mm (E/4)

Scissors

Tapestry needle

GAUGE

9 sts and 12 rows = 2"/5cm with Yarn A in Stockinette Stitch

10 sts and 12 rows = 2"/5cm with Yarn B in Rib Pattern

Always take time to check your gauge.

Instructions

LEG

With Yarn A and larger knitting needles, CO 48 (52, 56) sts.

Work in St st (k1 row, p1 row) for 54 (54, 58) rows. Work decs on rows 17 (17, 21), 31 (31, 35), 43 (43, 47), 53 (53, 57) as follows: K1, skp, k to last 3 sts, k2tog, k1.

There are now 40 (44, 48) sts on your needle. BO all sts.

TOP CUFF

With RS facing, Yarn B and smaller knitting needles, pick up and k48 (52, 56) sts, inserting the needle under back loop of CO sts.

Work in k2, p2 rib for 1 row. K the knits and p the purls for 11 (11, 15) more rows. BO in Rib st.

BOTTOM CUFF

With RS facing, Yarn B, and smaller knitting needles, pick up and k40 (44, 48) sts, inserting the needle under back loop of BO sts.

Work in k2, p2 rib for 1 row. K the knits and p the purls for 11 (11, 15) more rows. BO in Rib st.

SEAM

With RS facing and top close to you, fold legwarmer to bring right and left edges tog to form seam opening.

With Yarn C, and starting at the end close to you, insert hook downwards on right side of the seam opening. Ch 2 and insert hook downwards on left side of seam opening. Yarn over and pull yarn through corner st and st on the hook. (Figure 1)

*Ch 2, insert hook downwards in 2nd st of 2nd row along right side of the seam opening, and pull yarn through this st and st on the hook. Ch 2, insert hook downwards in 2nd st of the 2nd row along left side of the seam opening, and pull yarn through this st and st on the hook.

Rep from * until bottom of legwarmer. Cut yarn, tie ends, and hide tails.

This project was knit with

(A) 2 (3) balls of Gedifra Tecno Hair Lungo, heavy worsted weight, 100% polyamide yarn, 1¾oz/50g = approx 88yd/80m per ball, color #9715

(B) 2 balls of Schachenmayr Joana, chunky weight, 50% acrylic/50% new cool wool, 1¾oz/50g = approx 66yd/60m per ball, color #85

(C) 1 ball of Schachenmayr Mohana, chunky weight, 33% mohair/67% acrylic, 1¾oz/50g = approx 137yd/125m per ball, color #32

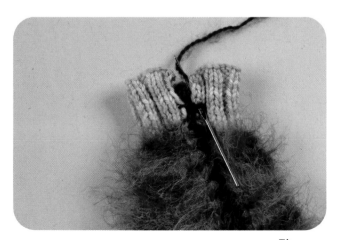

Figure 1

ENHANCEMENTS

Decorating socks with details such as cute faces, delicate crocheted ribbons, and leather pockets is a great way of dressing them up. Use these enhancements on the projects in the preceding pages, or integrate them into a pair of store-bought socks.

Crocheted Flower

This pretty flower makes a summery enhancement to any delicate pair of socks. You can add it to Dancing Queen Socks (page 24), or use it to embellish a pair of store-bought socks. Be sure to select a relatively light, delicate yarn for the flowers so that they don't weigh down the sock.

FINISHED MEASUREMENTS

2½"/6cm (stem); 1½"/4cm (flower with petals)

MATERIALS AND TOOLS

Yarn A **LIGHT 3** : 10yd/9m of Light weight yarn, cotton/acrylic, in green

Yarn B **LIGHT 3** : 10yd/9m of Light weight yarn, cotton/acrylic, in orange

Yarn C **LIGHT 3** : 10yd/9m of Light weight yarn, cotton/acrylic, in yellow

Crochet hook: 3.5 mm (E/4)
2 red beads, ½"/1cm in diameter
Sewing needle and thread
Scissors

Instructions

Choose the site of the flower and decide on the length of the stem. You'll begin at the bottom of the stem and work towards the flower.

STEM AND LEAVES

With RS facing, fold Yarn A and hold inside the sock. Hold hook outside the sock and pull yarn through where you want to begin the stem.

Sl st 6 in each 2nd row st towards top of sock in a winding direction for stem.

To make the bottom leaf, sl st 2 to the left, then sl st 2 to the right in adjacent row sts, ending in the 1st sl st of this leaf. (Figure 1)

Cont sl st upwards for another 4 sl sts (Figure 1) To make the next leaf, sl st 2 to the right, then sl st 2 to the left in adjacent row sts, ending in the 1st sl st of this leaf. Rep to desired length to flower center. Cut yarn, tie ends, and hide tails.

NOTE: *The flower on the 2nd sock should be a mirror image of the flower on the 1st sock, so make sure the stems and leaves are oriented in opposite directions.*

FLOWER CENTER

Fold Yarn B and hold inside the sock. Hold hook outside the sock and pull yarn through in last sl st of stem. Sl st 8 in a circle, so the last sl st is at the top of the stem. (Figure 2) Cut yarn leaving a 40"/1m tail, and pull yarn through.

Insert hook under 1st sl st of the circle, ch 1, then sc 1 under same st. Sc 2 under each following sl st of the circle. (Figure 3) End with sl st under 1st sc. Cut yarn, tie ends, and hide tails.

PETALS

With Yarn C, insert hook in 1st sc of center and ch 5, sl st into next sc. Rep sixteen times, until last sc of center. (Figure 4) End with sl st in 1st sc of the center. Cut yarn, tie ends, and hide tails.

BEADED CENTER

Sew a bead in the center of the flower using matching thread.

This project was knit with

(A) 1 ball of Schachenmayr Jazz, light weight, 50% cotton/50% acrylic yarn, 1¾oz/50g = approx 137yd/125m per ball, color #72

(B) 1 ball of Schachenmayr Jazz, light weight, 50% cotton/50% acrylic yarn, 1¾oz/50g = approx 137yd/125m per ball, color #26

(C) 1 ball of Schachenmayr Jazz, light weight, 50% cotton/50% acrylic yarn, 1¾oz/50g = approx 137yd/125m per ball, color #25

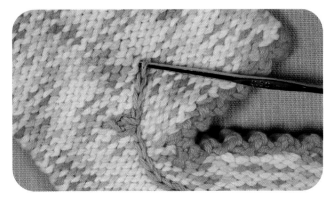

Figure 1

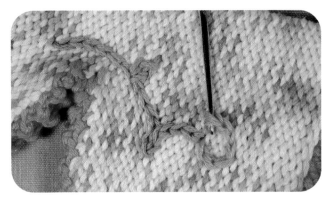

Figure 2

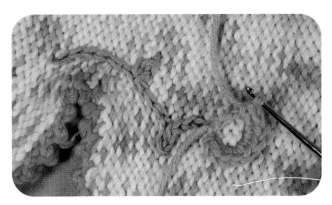

Figure 3

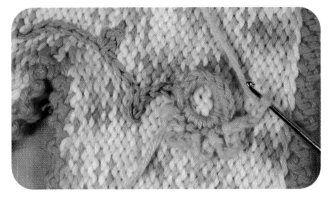

Figure 4

Lucky Leather Sock Pocket

Looking for a place to store your keys? How about a leather pocket that fits snuggly on your sock? This pocket is perfect on the Zingy Zigzag socks (page 37), but can be added to any pair of socks that is sturdy enough to support the leather.

FINISHED MEASUREMENTS

2½ x 2"/6 x 5cm

MATERIALS AND TOOLS

SUPER BULKY 6 2yd/2m of Super bulky weight yarn, wool/acrylic/polyamide, in army green

Crochet hook: 3.5 mm (E/4)

Tracing paper, pencil, and permanent marker

Scissors

Black leather piece, 4½ X 4"/12 X 10cm

Leather hole punch, 3 and 4mm holes

Black leather cord, 4"/10cm

Safety pin

Tapestry needle

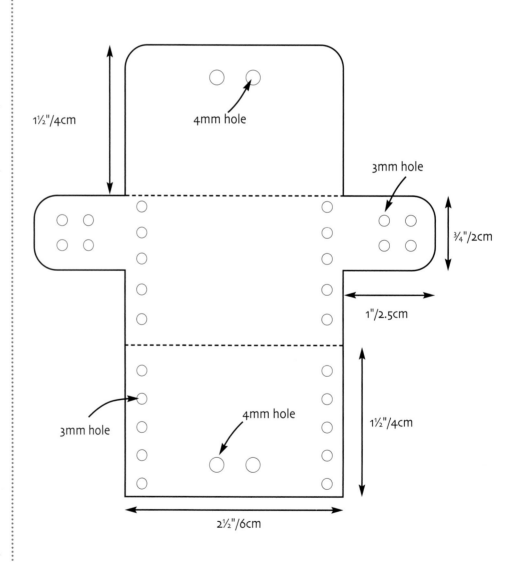

Pocket template

Instructions

PREPARING THE POCKET TEMPLATE

With the pencil, copy the pocket template (facing page) onto tracing paper and mark holes. Cut out, transfer to leather piece, trace with permanent marker, and cut out leather pocket. Punch holes as marked. Note that there are 4 mm holes at the top and bottom of the pocket (for stringing the leather cord), and 3mm holes everywhere else. Take care that the holes are evenly spaced, since they must be lined up to assemble the pocket. (Figure 1)

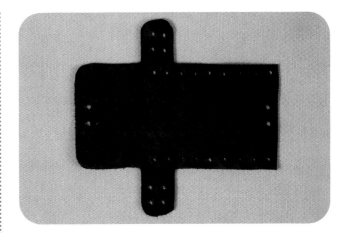

Figure 1

FOLDING THE POCKET

Fold the pocket along the dotted line on the bottom half, and string the leather cord through the 4mm holes at this end. Fold the pocket over and draw the ends of the cord through corresponding holes at the top. (Figure 2) Pull gently and tie in a loose knot. This will help secure the pocket as you crochet the sides.

With yarn and hook, sl st to connect holes along the sides of the pocket.

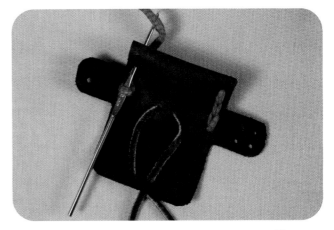

Figure 2

ATTACHING THE POCKET

Put sock on foot, decide where to position pocket, and mark with the safety pin.

Remove sock and sew on pocket with yarn by making two sets of crisscross stitches in the holes on either side of the pocket. (Figure 3)

Figure 3

This project was knit with

1 ball of Gedifra Shanina, super bulky weight, 30% wool/30% acrylic/40% polyamide, 1¾oz/50g = approx 82yd/75m per ball, color #5078

Hemp Leaf Ribbon

This lovely ribbon is elegant and dainty—just what's required to finish the Summer Net Socks (page 54). It can be added to any pair of socks; just be sure to affix the crocheted edging (facing page) to make the loops for holding the ribbon.

FINISHED MEASUREMENTS

40"/100cm

MATERIALS AND TOOLS

Yarn A **LIGHT 3** : 22yd/20m of Light weight yarn, cotton/acrylic, in light green

Yarn B **MEDIUM 4** : 22yd/20m of Medium weight yarn, cotton, in grey-beige

Crochet hook: 3.5 mm (E/4)

Scissors

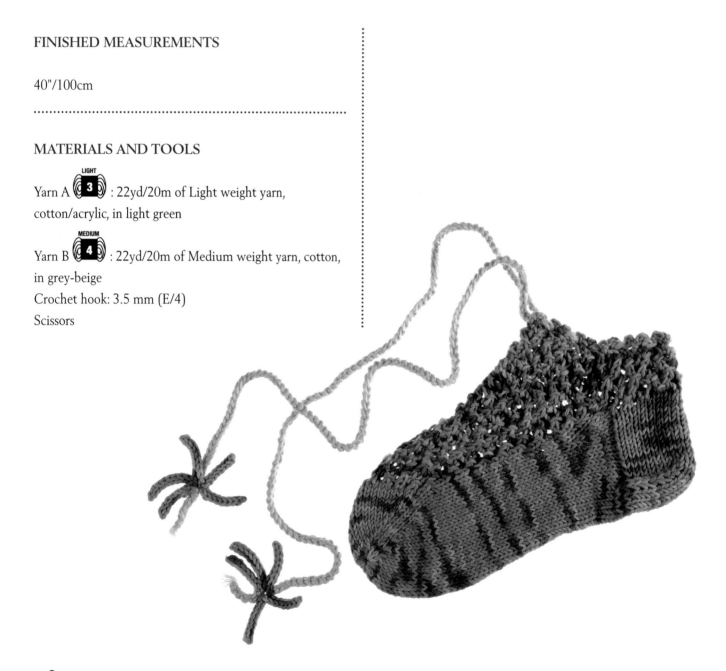

NOTE: *The leafy fringes at either end of this ribbon are much wider than the crocheted loops along the top of the sock, so string the ribbon through the loops before making the fringes.*

CROCHETED EDGING (for supporting ribbon)

Position sock with RS facing, gusset pointing up, and top away from you. With Yarn B, insert hook under 1st CO st and ch 4, sl st under 2nd CO st from hook. *Ch 4, sl st under every 2nd CO st from hook. Rep from * all around top of sock. Cut yarn, tie ends, and hide tails.

RIBBON

With 2 strands of Yarn A and hook, ch 240 sts or any desired length. Cut yarn, tie ends, and hide tails.

Insert the ribbon into loop at front middle of sock. Draw ribbon around sock and pull out at front middle of sock.

FRINGES

With Yarn B, insert hook into 8th ch from end of ribbon. Fold yarn, pull through st and *ch 7. Work back through these ch sts, making 7 sl sts. (Figure 1) Rep to make 4 more branches. Cut yarn, tie ends, and hide tails. Rep from * on other end of ribbon (Figure 2).

This project was knit with

(A) 1 ball of Schachenmayr Jazz, light weight, 50% cotton/50% acrylic yarn, 1¾oz/50g = approx 137yd/125m per ball, color #04

(B) 1 ball Gedifra Frisetto Color, worsted weight, 100% cotton, 1¾oz/50g = approx 109yd/100m per ball, color #8802

Figure 1

Figure 2

Pompon on a String

This pair of pompons, connected by a crocheted ribbon, is a perfect finish for the Wavy Sea Socks (page 58).

FINISHED MEASUREMENTS

12"/31cm

MATERIALS AND TOOLS

Yarn A **BULKY 5**: 33yd/30m of Bulky weight yarn, mohair/acrylic, in white

Yarn B **SUPER BULKY 6**: 22yd/20m of Bulky weight yarn, merino wool/acrylic/polyamide, in navy

Crochet hook: 3.5 mm (E/4)

Tracing paper, pencil, and permanent marker

Scissors

Large piece of cardboard

Tapestry needle

Safety pin

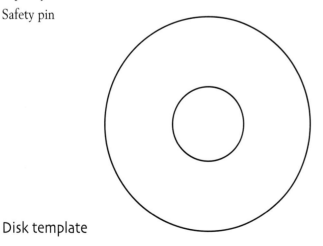

Disk template

Instructions

POMPONS

With the pencil, copy the disk template onto tracing paper. Cut out, transfer twice to cardboard with the permanent marker, and cut out cardboard disks.

NOTE: *The size of your pompon depends on the size of the disk. The thickness of the pompon depends on the size of the hole in the center of the disks. Take these two factors into account when preparing your disks, so you can make the pompons exactly as you want them.*

Lay cardboard disks on top of each other so that the holes in the center are lined up. Thread needle with 2 strands of Yarn A (or 1 strand each of Yarn A and Yarn B), and wrap the disks by drawing the thread up through the holes in the center of the disks and around the disk's outer edge. Wrap the yarn snuggly, so that the strands sit close together. Wrap until the hole is filled. (Figure 1)

Insert scissors between the discs and cut yarn all around (Figure 2). Cut a small piece of Yarn A and tie tightly around the middle of the pompon, between the disks. Cut yarn, leaving a 4"/10cm tail for sewing the pompon onto the crocheted ribbon.

Remove cardboard disks and trim yarn to make pompon even (Figure 3). Fluff up with a little steam.

Follow same instructions to make three more pompons. (You'll attach two pompons to each sock.)

RIBBON

With 2 strands of Yarn A and hook, ch 80 sts. Cut yarn, tie ends, and hide tails.

Thread the tail from the pompom onto the needle and sew one pompom onto either end of the ribbon.

Put sock on foot, decide where to position pompoms, and mark with safety pin. Remove the sock and place the ribbon so it hangs evenly on either side. Sew the ribbon onto the sock with a few simple stitches and tie into a bow.

Follow same instructions to make another ribbon. Attach a pompom to both ends of both ribbons and sew onto sock (Figure 4).

This project was knit with

(A) 1 ball of Schachenmayr Mohana, chunky weight, 33% mohair/67% acrylic, 1¾oz/50g = approx 137yd/125m per ball, color #01

(B) 1 ball of Gedifra Boheme, bulky weight, 43% merino wool/43% acrylic/14% polyamide yarn, 1¾oz/50g = approx 109yd/100m per ball, color #1868

Figure 1

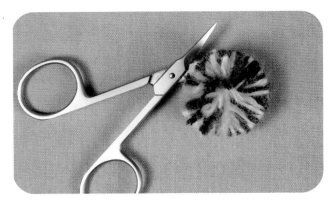

Figure 2

Figure 3

Figure 4

Funny Bunnies

Affix these fluffy animals to Cute as a Bunny Cuffed Socks (page 62). Be sure to use fluffy yarn for the muzzle, as it makes the animal look particularly cute (and simplifies the crocheting).

FINISHED MEASUREMENTS

Diameter: 1½"/4cm

MATERIALS AND TOOLS

Yarn A **BULKY 5** : 22yd/20m of Bulky weight yarn, polyamide, in black and white

or

Yarn B **BULKY 5** : 22yd/20m of Bulky weight yarn, polyamide, in apricot

Crochet hook: 3.5 mm (E/4)

Scissors

Tapestry needle

Sewing needle and thread

2 round brown buttons, ½"/1.3cm in diameter

4 blue beads, ¼"/0.6cm in diameter

2 brown leather laces, 4"/10cm long

Safety pin

Instructions

FACE

With Yarn A (Yarn B) and hook, ch 4, sl st in 1st ch to join sts into a circle. Ch 1, sc 8 in center of circle. Sl st in 1st sc. Sc 2 in each sc around until disk is about 1½"/4cm in diameter. (Figure 1)

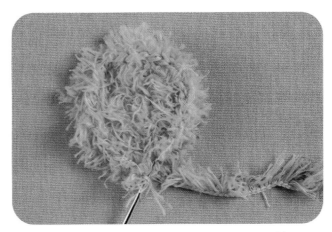

Figure 1

EARS

Row 1: To make first ear, ch 12, sc 1 in next sc from hook. Then make the second ear with ch 12, sc 1 in next sc from hook. (Figure 2)

Row 2: Ch 1, sc 12 in center of second ear, sl st into sc between ears, ch 1, sc 12 in center of first ear. End with sl st. Cut yarn, tie ends, and hide tails.

Find the middle of the face and sew on a brown button. Sew on 2 blue beads just above the button. Pass the leather lace through one ear and tie in a bow (Figure 3).

Figure 2

ATTACHING THE BUNNY

Put sock on foot, fold over cuffs, decide where to position bunny, and mark with safety pin. Remove sock and sew on bunny.

NOTE: *Bunny will be sewn onto WS of sock—this becomes RS when the cuff is folded over.*

This project was knit with

(A) 1 ball of Schachenmayr Cassiopeia, chunky weight, 100% polyamide, 1¾oz/50g = approx 77yd//70m per ball, color #26

(B) 1 ball of Schachenmayr Cassiopeia, chunky weight, 100% polyamide, 1¾oz/50g = approx 77yd//70m per ball, color #90

Figure 3

Rosebud Ribbon

This ribbon is decorated with tiny crocheted circles that resemble rosebuds at either end. Use it to wrap up Sally's Seashell Crocheted Socks (page 99). Make the rosebuds in identical colors, or use different colors to add a touch of asymmetry.

FINISHED MEASUREMENTS

24"/61cm

MATERIALS AND TOOLS

Yarn A **MEDIUM 4**: 22yd/20m of Medium weight yarn, nylon/acrylic/kid mohair, in dark or light blue

Yarn B **MEDIUM 4**: 22yd/20m of Medium weight yarn, nylon/acrylic/kid mohair, in apricot

Yarn C **MEDIUM 4**: 5yd/5m of 4 medium weight yarn, nylon/acrylic/kid mohair, in coral
Crochet hook: 3.5 mm (E/4)
Scissors

Instructions

NOTE: *The rosebuds at either end of this ribbon may be wider than the holes in the sock, so string the ribbon around the sock before making the rosebuds.*

RIBBON

With 2 strands of Yarn A (Yarn C) and hook, ch 100 sts or any desired length. Cut yarn, tie ends, and hide tails.

Insert the ribbon into 3rd round of shells at the front middle of the sock. Draw ribbon around sock by weaving it through the middle of each shell and between shells. Pull out at front middle of sock.

ROSEBUDS

With Yarn B, insert hook into last ch of ribbon and pull through, *ch 3, sl st in 1st ch, sc in same ch of ribbon.

Rep from * seven times.

End with sl st in 1st ch from beg of rnd.

Cut yarn, tie ends, and hide tails.

With Yarn C (Yarn A), insert hook into last ch at the other end of the ribbon and make another rosebud.

This project was knit with

(A) 1 ball of Schachenmayr Kid Light, Aran weight, 35% nylon/35% acrylic/30% kid mohair, 1¾oz/50g = approx 328yd/300m per ball, color #65 or #69
(B) 1 ball of Schachenmayr Kid Light, Aran weight, 35% nylon/35% acrylic/30% kid mohair, 1¾oz/50g = approx 328yd/300m per ball, color #27
(C) 1 ball of Schachenmayr Kid Light, Aran weight, 35% nylon/35% acrylic/30% kid mohair, 1¾oz/50g = approx 328yd/300m per ball, color #34

Figure 1

Sole templates

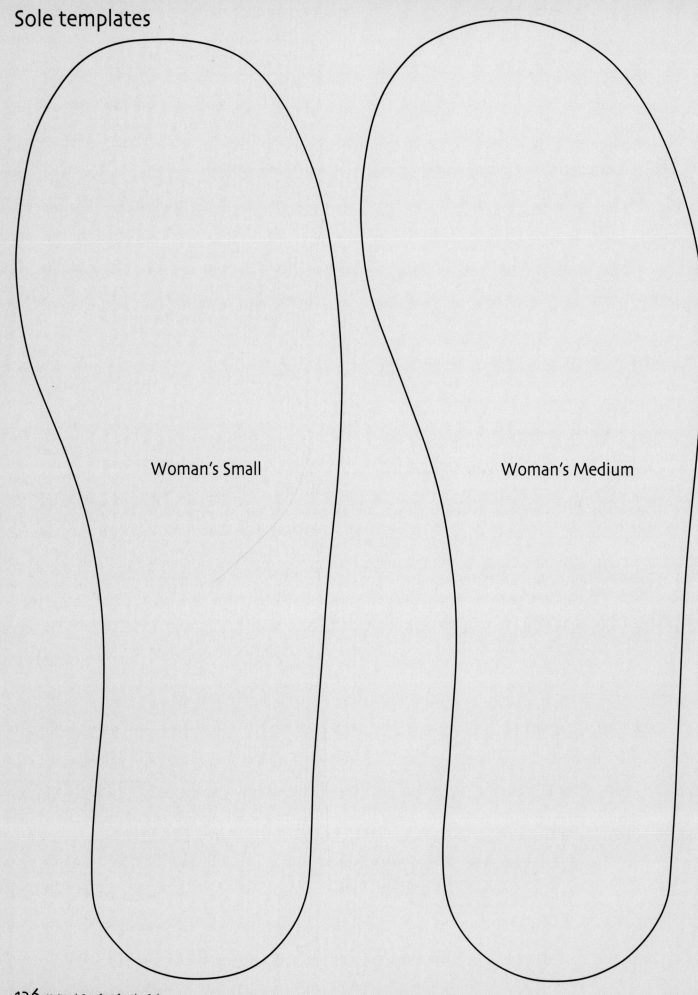

Woman's Small

Woman's Medium

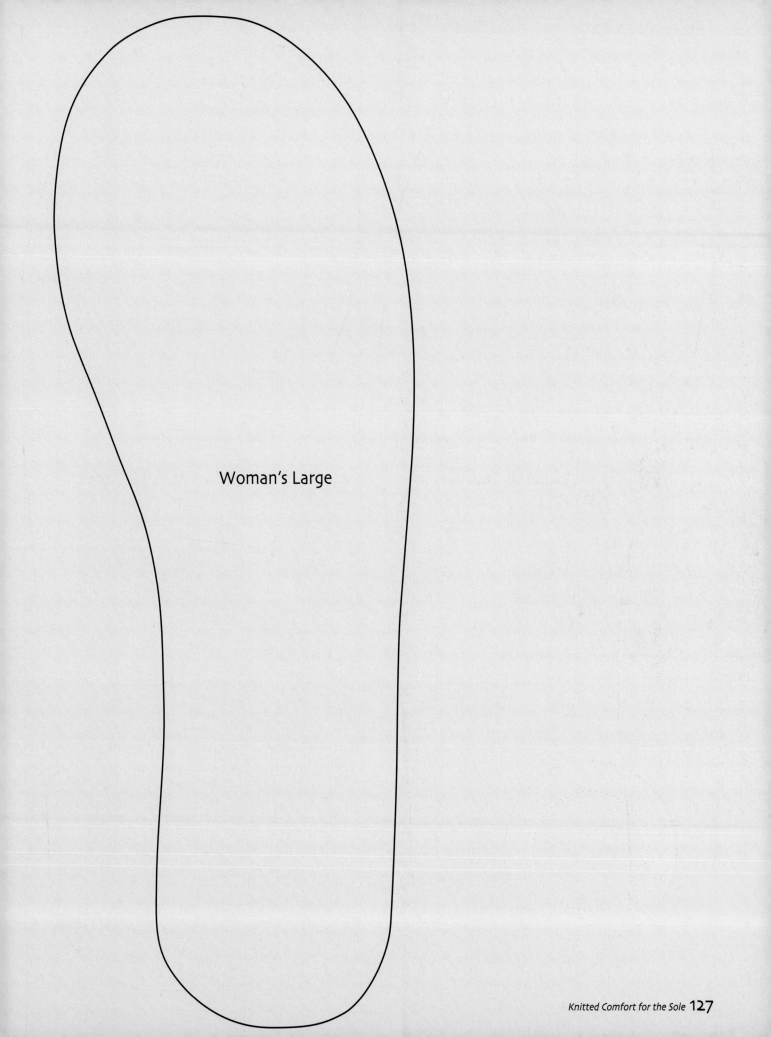

Woman's Large